PANKRA

THE TRADITIONAL GREEK COMBAT SPORT AND MODERN MIXED MARTIAL ART

JIM ARVANITIS

PALADIN PRESS · BOULDER, COLORADO

Pankration: The Traditional Greek Combat Sport and Modern Mixed Martial Art
by Jim Arvanitis

Copyright © 2003 by Jim Arvanitis

ISBN 13: 978-1-58160-397-2
Printed in the United States of America

Published by Paladin Press, a division of
Paladin Enterprises, Inc.
Gunbarrel Tech Center
7077 Winchester Circle
Boulder, Colorado 80301 USA
+1.303.443.7250

Direct inquiries and/or orders to the above address.

Visit our Web site at www.paladin-press.com

TABLE OF CONTENTS

WARNING

Neither the author nor the publisher assumes any responsibility
for the use or misuse of information contained in this book.
It is presented *for academic study only.*

ACKNOWLEDGMENTS

Participants: Brandon Arvanitis, Bryson Arvanitis, Eric Hill, James Hines, Nick Hines, and M. Nash.

Photographs by Chrys Gardner, Katherine Ayoob, Richard Balboni, and David Lowden.

Computer-generated graphics by Bryson Arvanitis.

Illustrations by Jim Arvanitis.

DEDICATION

To my family for their continued support and encouragement throughout the years, and to my Greek ancestors for developing the roots of this fascinating martial art and combat sport. Bravo!

INTRODUCTION

The martial arts are as old as man himself. For every country on the planet, a unique form of fighting has been created that is indigenous to that particular culture. Greek *pankration* is among the oldest of these, having been well documented before the coming of Christ, and whose practice applied to both athletics and warfare. An original part of the earliest Olympic Games, pankration has influenced modern combat competition throughout the world to a degree that few of today's practitioners are aware of. The popular Ultimate Fighting Championships and other similar mixed-martial arts events are modeled after the ancient Greek combat sport.

It is not the intent of this book to serve as a how-to manual on learning pankration techniques, but rather to provide the martial arts enthusiast with an overall look at what this essential part of Greek combat once was and what it is today. While there have been excellent accounts of Greece's fighting sports in prior works, none can be considered a complete treatment of pankration. This book emphasizes the concepts and basic skills of modern pankration. It also covers the history of Grecian combat, its role in the very first Panhellenic festivals, and its influence on other forms of fighting around the globe, including the recent trend in no-holds-barred (NHB) bouts.

In truth the original pankration is no longer with us. Due to a number of factors, it died out thousands of years ago. In the late 1960s, it became my passion to redesign the ancient sport and bring recognition to my Greek ancestors for their achievement. In addition to being a disciplined athlete, I have always been an avid researcher of sorts. This became the focus of my first contact with pankration, which occurred while I was investigating the origins of systematized fighting methods. Although I had studied boxing, wrestling, and various self-defense styles, my strong ethnic ties were a factor in discovering information that was indeed relevant, though unknown, to the martial arts world at the time. Thus, I began the process of eventually rebuilding the defunct sport from its ashes into its modern derivative from what little remained. For me, ancient Greece's contribution to the pool of martial arts knowledge was immense and not to be ignored.

I also modified the pronunciation of the term *pankration*, preferring to anglicize it as "pan-cray-shun" as opposed to the current native-Greek *pagratio*. Other than those who have directly studied either with me or my affiliates, anyone using the former expression is blatantly imitating my alteration. After all, for more than two decades there was no one other than me and my small circle of followers exclusively training under this personalized label.

Structurally, modern pankration is patterned after the original, integrating striking and grappling techniques in what was among the very first forms of mixed martial arts. Although it was formerly the name for a competitive event, its descendant had become an eclectic composite, gleaning the best elements from a number of sources.

Another objective was to assimilate the ancient concepts into a comprehensive art. *Mu tau* became yet another name for this creation, and modern sport pankration was the core nucleus of its unarmed curriculum. It is pertinent to understanding here that mu tau is not a "style" of pankration. Mu tau, itself, is a modern Greek-inspired martial art, a complete system of hand-to-hand and armed combat methodologies, scientific training, and a deeply rooted cultural base extracted from Hellenic history, philosophy, and mythology. Modern pankration is actually a specialized branch of mu tau.

Needless to say, this became a lifelong commitment. History, concepts, and technique, in that order, became my guide, or "blueprint," in this process. I had found that most of today's Western and Asian combat styles contained techniques that indirectly were derived from pankration through the passing of time. In fact, most of the modern hand techniques used in Western boxing and the Oriental martial arts can be found in the archaeological record of vases, wall paintings, and sculptures left behind by the ancient Greeks. Thus, in studying a diversity of techniques, both of Greek influence and of other styles, I attempted to fill the void that was left by the departed sport.

In the early 1970s when, pankration was first exposed to the martial arts community, it received cries of criticism from the "classical establishment." These individuals, bound by their devotion to the more accepted styles of karate, tae kwon do, and kung fu, condemned Greek combat sport as a "savage, barbaric practice." Perhaps, their arrogance and lack of comprehension served to cloud their vision of where the martial arts were headed in the 1990s. Today, of course, the effectiveness of purely upright combat systems is obvious. In the arena of limited-rules contests competitors must be more open to the evolution of the arts. Yet this is nothing new to the pankratiast, for his ancestors had been practicing a similar approach to combat thousands of years before.

With the current interest in total fighting proficiency, there are many individuals alleging to be practicing pankration. Although it is certainly gratifying to see its global growth, what is interesting to note is that before my introduction of pankration some 30 years ago, there were few, if any, martial artists even remotely familiar with it. Pankration meant nothing more to them than some exotic European pastry. For example, one well-known karate instructor who just happened to be of Greek descent purchased one of my earlier books and, days later, was teaching a pankration style bearing his name in his dojos. There are also those groups who merely use pankration as nothing more than a convenient label for their amalgam of techniques. However, modern pankration is much more than this.

Even in present-day Greece, pankration was not mentioned until Greek karate practitioners, inspired by a new sense of patriotism, orchestrated a movement to begin using the term again. But this was not until 1995, some 20 years after I appeared in the landmark cover story of *Black Belt* magazine. Interestingly enough, few of my detractors have ever offered credit where it is due, yet the fact remains that none of them existed throughout the 1960s, 1970s, and into the 1980s.

Sadly enough this is not unusual conduct in the martial arts nowadays. Honor has taken a backseat to dishonesty in many cases. It seems it is justifiable for some to adopt the current buzz word, dream up an impressive but unsubstantiated background, and then ride on the publicity that has been conveniently established before. Others even go so far as to boast that they are "carrying the torch of Greece's legacy" or "[do] more for the sport than anyone else." Yet regardless of their ramblings and arguments in defense of their claims, pankration was not a subject of interest before 1973. These quoted statements are not purely a matter of unwarranted arrogance, but a matter of record.

Although the roots and basic framework of ancient pankration remain intact, its techniques and training reflect kineseological developments of our progressive culture. Technically pankration is a mixture of boxing and wrestling that includes kicking and submission holds. Its modern descendant has many points in common with several grappling styles, as well as with Thai kickboxing (Muay Thai) and even French savate. What is important here is that martial arts, on a physical level, are more alike than dissimilar. The major differences are in strategy; that is, whether a style is oriented toward waging combat from an upright position or on the ground, or whether it favors grappling or striking.

In pankration a student is offered the best of both worlds. He is prepared to defend himself in any possible situation, be it against one adversary or many, in either an unarmed or armed conflict. Much depends on the individual's body type, as well as the physical build and reactions of his opponent. For example, it would never be prudent to exchange blows with a better boxer than you. In this case, it might be wiser to go to the ground and grapple. But in a situation where you are facing two or more attackers, it would be more reasonable to remain on your feet and use striking skills. These are not radical new ways of thinking about combat, just common sense. Pragmatic and functional are the key principles of the pankration philosophy.

The *palaistra* (classical Greek for wrestling school) is found in increasing numbers in the United States and Canada, and there are reportedly thousands of active practitioners throughout Europe and in other parts of the world. Greece, France, and Spain each have their own government-backed organizations and conduct contests regularly. When Athens became the host site for the 2004 Olympics, a movement was inititiated to enter pankration as a "demo" sport. Despite these efforts, the sport was denied admission by the International Olympic Committee.

Although pankration has been used as a model for many mixed martial arts contests around the globe, one must not lose sight of the fact that it is a product of the Western world. It is *not* an Asian development, be it Japanese, Chinese, Korean, etc. Pankration comes from ancient Greece. Nor have I invented a new "style" of pankration. On the contrary, I have brought an awareness to a very old practice and updated it accordingly. Without question, pankration has a long and proven history. From its legends that rival the mythology of the gods to its adaptations for today's competitive arenas and for personal defense, the all-powers combat form of the Greeks has come full circle into the new millennium.

Jim (Demetrios) Arvanitis
May 2003

CHAPTER 1

HISTORY OF HELLENIC MARTIAL ARTS

Greece is well known for its many achievements in the pre–Christian era. Along with literature, science, art, and philosophy, Greek military and athletic developments are without equal. Credit belongs to the Greeks for both the word *athlete* and the ideal it expresses. It is also the Greek soldier who would represent the standard for the rest of the world to follow for centuries. It was during Greece's classical age (7th to 4th centuries B.C.) that athletics and combat sports, in particular, would make their marks in Greek history and Western civilization.

There were several reasons for the popularity of Hellenic combat during this time. Most important was the need of the city-state, or *polis*, to prepare its citizens for warfare. Second was the worship of health, beauty, and strength—the real religion of the Greeks. The ancient Greeks were as health-conscious as many Americans are today. Last but not least was the characteristic Greek love for competition and victory, which highly trained athletes aspired to in the sport festivals of the ancient world. These included the games at Olympia and Delphi (Pythian festival), Corinth (Isthmian festival), Nemea, and other Panhellenic events. Men who won at all four festivals received the special title of *periodonikes*. The classic Greek athlete was akin to his modern counterpart who practices his chosen style for purposes of personal defense, health, and self-expression.

Although many countries claim the origin of the martial arts, ancient Greece has the best historical records substantiating its developments. Much of this information comes from old vase paintings and sculptures depicting early Greek warriors in combat, as well as quotes from famous poets and philosophers. Many historians believe that early unarmed- and armed-combat techniques entered Greece from Egypt. Greece then modified and refined these techniques, which later found their way to India.

The martial arts practiced by the ancient Greeks were first established for military training. The unarmed aspect was called *panmachia*, which meant "total fight." Later, competitions were created to simulate this battlefield combat. These sports date back to the earliest Olympic Games, which commenced in 776 B.C. at Olympia. From this date on, the games were staged every four years until A.D. 391. While military training familiarized the Greeks with the fighting arts, the spirit of competition spurred them on to mastery. The three major combative sports included in the Games were wrestling, boxing, and the brutal pankration. The Greeks referred to these as the "heavy events," because, due to the lack of weight divisions in antiquity, they became the domain of the large and strong. These forms of hand-to-hand fighting are the earliest thoroughly documented combative disciplines and stand out as the probable predecessors of today's martial arts styles.

PALE (GREEK WRESTLING)

Wrestling is Greece's oldest combat sport, having been introduced into the Olympics of 708 B.C. Wrestling appealed deeply to the ancients and was highly valued as a form of weaponless military training. The poet Pindar claimed that the Olympic Games came into existence as a result of a wrestling match between the gods Zeus and Cronus. Like all classic Greek athletes, the wrestlers wore no clothing and often oiled themselves to keep dirt out of their pores. Powder was then added to their hands to ensure a good grip.

There were two distinct versions of the sport, differing according to the holds employed and the methods of deciding the victor of a contest. *Kato pale*, or ground wrestling, was decided when one competitor acknowledged defeat by raising his right hand with the index finger pointed. In *orthia pale*, or upright-style wrestling, the objective was simply to throw the opponent to the ground. Three falls constituted a loss for a fighter, with the winner declared the *triakter*. Some considered the Greek stand-up wrestling style to be the most practical unarmed training for war. The *hoplites*, or Greek soldiers, could not afford to get involved in lengthy ground combat during battle, so throwing the enemy to the ground while remaining on their feet seemed the most effective tactical method to many of the early Greek purists.

Ancient Greek wrestling had no time limits and no defined ring or fighting area. It also lacked weight classifications: every contestant entered the tough open division, which placed the smaller man at an extreme disadvantage. The contest consisted of the best out of three falls. A fall was defined as touching the ground with the knees. Once a wrestler threw his opponent, he would pin his foe's shoulders, thereby winning the contest.

Much of the action allowed leg and shoulder throws, holds, and foot sweeps. Strikes of any kind were illegal. Sacrifice throws, ground fighting, and finishing techniques were well known but generally reserved for the pankration, or "all-powers," event.

Ancient Greek *pale* bouts commenced with the wrestlers'

Shoulder throw. (Greek vase, circa 500 B.C.)

The "heave," a throwing technique that often followed a reverse waistlock. (Greek bronze, Hellenic era.)

The offensive wrestler applies a reverse waistlock and prepares to hoist his opponent feet first into the air. (Greek vase, 525-510 B.C.)

The great champion Theseus counters his rival's attack with a waistlock and prepares to throw him. (Greek vase, 500 B.C.)

him down on his head. This might be called a "pile driver" in modernized wrestling.

Wrestlers trained at either of two facilities, the *palaistrai* or the *gymnopaidia,* both of which were centers for the practice of the fighting arts. Most palaestrae were buildings within the city walls, much like large houses. They were owned by private individuals and were equipped with dressing rooms, lounges, and store rooms that contained the oil and powder applied by the wrestlers during practice. Training was held in the center courtyards, which were normally covered with fine sand. The athletes were first taught basic throwing techniques and maneuvers, which were followed by more sophisticated combinations.

As a means of physical development, wrestling was designed to teach not only grappling skills but also an esthetic sense of balance, grace, and finesse. This emphasis on "clean" technique had a definite impact on the manner in which competitive wrestling was conducted; the Greeks sought not only victory but victory with grace and style. Poor technique was unacceptable.

In contrast to the palaistra, the gymnopaidia was under the ownership of the *polis* and was administered by publicly appointed officials. All types of athletic endeavors were played in this spacious outdoor sports ground located outside the city. The gymnopaidia also had wrestling facilities but served as a center of boxing and pankration training as well. Special trainers were employed to coach citizens and athletes. Training in empty-hand fighting techniques was provided by the paidotribes and gymnastes, while armed combat was taught by the *hoplomachos* (weapons specialists), usually to the wealthy.

Wrestlers struggling on the ground. (Greek vase, 525–510 B.C.)

seeking control of each other's wrists or neck as a prelude to follow-up offensives. Another means of engagement was the underhook, a hold obtained by grasping underneath the adversary's shoulder in preparation for a throw.

A number of vase paintings show attempts to take an opponent down by tackling his legs or clinching him about the midsection. One extremely effective technique was the waistlock, which was applied from either the front, much like a bear hug, or behind one's foe. Being caught in this hold was a sign of serious disadvantage. It often was followed by a maneuver known as the "heave." After defending against a leg takedown, the wrestler gripped his opponent around the back of the waist, hoisted him feet first into the air, and then slammed

5

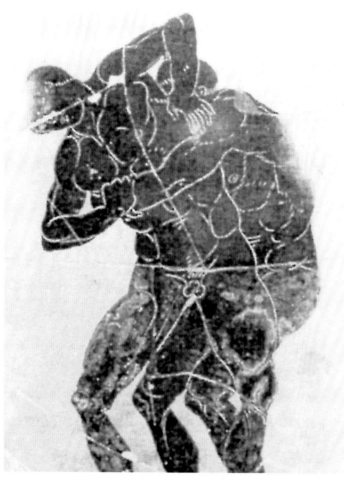

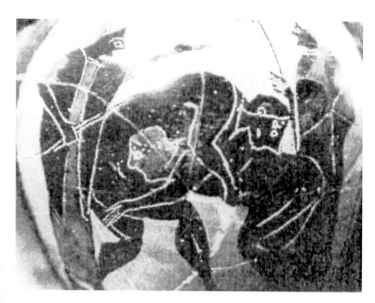

Against a leg tackle, the wrestler on the left sprawls his opponent by gripping him about the waist while dropping his weight forward. (Greek vase, 6th century B.C.)

Waistlock from the rear flank, which the defending wrestler is attempting to break by tearing at the encircling arm. (Greek vase, 360–359 B.C.)

Theseus counters a leg tackle by Kerkyon by catching him under the arms, putting him in excellent position to either throw his opponent or apply a front headlock. (Greek vase, 460–450 B.C.)

A classic match between Theseus and Kerkyon: Theseus applies a headlock as Kerkyon attempts to grip the leg. (Greek vase, 510 B.C.)

The gymnopaidia also served as the training place for the *epheboi*, young men in their later teens who were required to have two years of intensive military, athletic, and physical education. In addition to unarmed combat and weapons training, the young Spartans learned the *pyrrhic*, a dancelike exercise during which the trainees, armed with shields and javelins, performed different offensive movements and defenses. This form of training was considered so effective that Socrates once remarked that "the best dancer is also the best warrior."

The pyrrhic is included in this passage from the *Laws* by the great philosopher Plato (approximately 427–347 B.C.):

The war dance has a different character, and may be properly called the Pyrrhic; it depicts the motions of

Wrestler on the right prepares to throw his opponent by grasping his wrist and underhooking his left arm. (Greek vase, 366 B.C.)

The grappler on the left has secured a headlock on his rival and prepares to throw him over his hip. (Greek vase, 425 B.C.)

The wrestler on the right attempts a hip throw but is foiled by the opponent's tight waistlock. (Greek vase, 520 B.C.)

Kato pale, or ground wrestling, was more reserved for the pankration, although groundwork was frequently employed in ancient Greek wrestling. (Greek vase, 360–359 B.C.)

eluding blows and shots of every kind by various devices of swerving, yielding ground, leaping from the ground or crouching; as well as the contrary motions which lead to a posture of attack, and aim at the reproduction of the shooting of arrows, casting of darts, and dealing in all kinds of blows. In these dances the upright, well-braced posture which represents the good body and good mind, and in which the bodily members are in the main kept straight, is the kind of attitude we pronounce right, that which depicts their contrary, wrong.

Greek dancing was closely connected with religion and formed part of all religious festivals and processions. The

7

dance was dramatic and imitative and exercised every part of the body. Some dances were definitely athletic or military in character. In Sparta the dancers imitated all movements of wrestling.

Perhaps the most famous and successful of the Olympic wrestling champions was Milo of Croton. After winning his first Olympic victory in boy's wrestling, he achieved five wins in the men's division. At the age of 40 he attempted a bid for a sixth title, only to be defeated by a younger man.

Wrestling did not rank as a brutal combat sport by the Greeks. Few stories present an image of it as being particularly bloody and violent or having been the cause of numerous fatalities to athletes. These characteristics were more of the boxing and pankration events.

PYXMACHIA (GREEK BOXING)

Boxing appears to have been first practiced in the Minoan civilization of Crete around 3000 to 1200 B.C. The fighters wore protective headgear, and there is speculation that kicking was an integral part of the art's techniques. One Cretan vase bears testimony to this by showing a fallen fighter kicking upward at his opponent. According to mythology Apollo invented boxing. He was said to have defeated and killed Phorbas, a boxer who urged travelers through Delphi to compete against him. Philostratus, however, claimed that Greek boxing was pioneered by the Spartans.

Known as *pyxmachia,* or simply *pyx,* Greek boxing was initially introduced into the Olympic Games of 688 B.C. The first victor was Onomastus of Smyrna, who was said to have drawn up the rules for the sport. Like wrestling, boxing bouts had no weight divisions, and the action was conducted in an open area rather than a roped-off ring as in today's matches. Blows were allowed with both the fist and the open hand; few punches were prohibited. Surprisingly, there was no rule against striking a downed opponent.

There were also no rounds or time limits, with many contests continuing until one contestant either was knocked out or raised his right hand as a sign of defeat. The pyx contest could therefore be a waiting game and a test of stamina. If a long match occurred without the declaration of a clear-cut winner, both fighters could opt for *klimax.* In klimax, an agreement was made to trade blows until one or the other dropped, and neither man would attempt to block or evade the attacks. The story of Creugas and Damoxenus illustrates this type of fighting arrangement. In 400 B.C. at the Nemean Games, these two combatants, one from Syracuse, the other from Epidamnus, struggled into the dusk without a decision. They finally agreed to permit each other to strike one last blow, unresisted, to settle the issue. Creugas struck first, punching Damoxenus solidly in the head. Damoxenus, however, weathered the blow and ordered his rival to raise his left arm. He then struck Creugas with his open hand, spearlike, with such force that it penetrated Creugas' side, killing him instantly.

The Greek boxer's stance featured a relatively wide spacing of the feet, with the chin down and the hands held high to

As the boxer on the right prepares to deliver an uppercut, his opponent has landed first with an open-hand strike to the face. (Greek vase, 6th century B.C.)

protect the face. The front hand was normally extended, sometimes open, and was employed for both defense and attack. The rear hand was used for hooks and uppercuts. Chopping blows to the top of the head, using the bottom of the closed fist, were also popular. The favorite targets for blows included the point of the chin, the bridge of the nose, and the sensitive nerve centers surrounding the ears. There is also evidence that blows to the groin were permitted.

Many boxing technicians were classified as "headhunters," aiming their punches to the head and face, although the Greeks were fully aware of the effectiveness of a sustained body attack. The body, being larger and less mobile than the head, was logistically a better target for slowing an opponent down, thereby exposing the head for finishing blows. Evasive footwork and defensive skills were not highly developed at this time, the fighters relying more on their ability to withstand punishment and dish out more than their adversaries. Backing away from blows was considered a sign of cowardice. The victor of a match often emerged bruised and bloodied but in far better shape than his defeated rival.

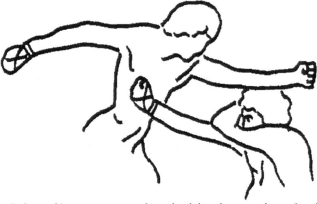

Body punching was not as popular as head shots, but many boxers found the technique effective in taking the fight out of their opponents.

The boxer on the left has scored a knockdown with a powerful left punch. (Greek vase, 6th century B.C.)

Ancient Greek boxer wearing himantes *on his fists. (Greek statue, 1st century B.C.)*

The boxers fought barehanded at first but later wrapped *himantes,* straps of soft oxhide, around their hands to strengthen their wrists and steady their fingers. Himantes were wrapped around the first knuckles of the fingers and then run diagonally across the palm onto the back of the hand, leaving the thumb uncovered. Then they were tied around the wrist or forearm. The forms of these hand wraps evolved with straps of harder leather added around the knuckles to make the blows even more devastating.

Alterations to the himantes brought about significant changes in the techniques of the sport. When the thongs were softer, boxing required skill, agility, and good technique with a particular emphasis on offense. The introduction of the sharp thongs slowed the contest, with the boxers paying greater attention to defense. Skill gradually became secondary to brute force.

The Roman invention of the *caestus,* a glove weighted with iron and with protruding spikes, transformed Greek boxing into an inhuman and deadly contest. In Rome it was not unusual for such public brutality—as it was the rule rather than the exception—to satisfy the spectators' thirst for gore and violence. This alteration, however, diminished the skill and grace that the Greeks had come to admire in their athletes. Rarely, if ever, did a true Greek pugilist participate in the savage gladiatorial arenas of Rome, even though they were often tempted by higher purses and positions in the powerful Roman empire. As such, combat between slaves became more popular than the athletic skills of those who were free.

Boxing competition was fierce, with the prime objective being to hurt one's opponent. There was little evidence of sportsmanship or respect displayed between fighters, with no traditional handshake before the bout or hug afterward. Punching power, even in the absence of skill, often secured victory for the fighter. The young pugilist Glaukos of Karystos won his first Olympic attempt on the strength of his punch, even after receiving numerous injuries at the hands of more skillful opponents. It is interesting to note that Glaukos later gained fame for his sparring skill, no doubt the result of his narrow and painful first Olympic victory, which must have convinced him to improve his technique.

Roman pugilist wearing the deadly caestus. (Roman bronze statue.)

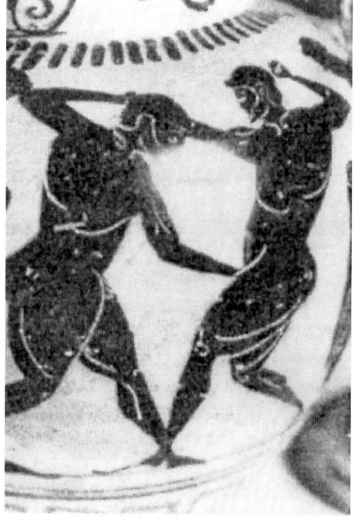

Boxer striking his opponent's groin area. (Greek vase, 6th century B.C.*)*

Boxers trained in a specially equipped room in the palaistra known as the *korykeion*, which featured various types of striking balls (*korykos*) suspended from the beams of the ceiling. This equipment was used by the Greek boxer in much the same manner as a modern boxer uses a striking bag for punching. The korykos was a wineskin filled with fig seeds, meal, or sand, and was hung at head level. The boxer would hit it with full force and allow it to slam him in the torso upon its rebound to toughen his midsection. The medical writer Antyllus provided a description of a heavy bag workout:

> Those undergoing training use both hands, at first gently, then more vigorously, so that they attack it as it swings away, and when it swings back at them they give ground as they are thrust out of the way by its force. Lastly they punch it away beyond arm's reach . . . with a final effort after doing it all the violence they can, they hit away so hard that if they were not very careful they would be thrown off their feet by the

rebound. . . . So it [the bag] can make the body muscular and give it tone, and it is a powerful exercise for the shoulders and the whole frame.

Other methods of training by Greek boxers included light sparring practice (*akrocheirismos*). The fighters wore padded gloves (*sphairai*) and earguards (*amphotides*) to protect the hands and head against injury. Boxers were also fond of a primitive form of shadowboxing (*skiamachia*), which sometimes was accompanied by the playing of the flute, since the ancients recognized the importance of rhythm in their physical activities.

Among ancient Greece's most famous boxers was Diagoras of Rhodes. He was recognized for his many victories but was even more renowned for his personal boxing style. Diagoras never ducked away from a blow and always played by the rules of the sport. Fans adored the grace and dignity he displayed in his bouts.

At the 83rd Olympiad, Diagoras watched his sons attain victories in both the boxing and pankration competitions. In celebration of their accomplishment, his sons placed their crowns on his head and carried him on their shoulders to the cheers of the crowd. To Diagoras, this was his most glorious moment, and while contemplating this, a voice from the crowd advised him to die now since there was nothing left but to ascend to Olympus and become a god. Ironically, Diagoras, while still held by his sons, dropped his head and quietly expired.

Another famed boxer, Melankomas of Caria, had an unusual fighting style that earned him countless victories. He was never injured and never hurt any of his opponents. It was his belief that to injure another or be injured yourself was to lack bravery. In many of his bouts, Melankomas would present such an elusive target that his opponents would become either so frustrated or exhausted that they would give up and admit defeat. What was so remarkable about his performance was that he never struck a single blow at them.

Theogenes, an early 5th-century boxer and pankratiast, who hailed from the island of Thasos, reportedly scored the greatest number of festival wins. With as many as 1,400 victories, he won distinction as one of Greece's most revered athletic heroes with two Olympic crowns, three Delphic boxing championships, a number of boxing victories at the Isthmus, and as many as nine Nemean boxing triumphs. As might be expected, Theogenes' history is full of legend and folklore, and he was worshipped as a deity after his death.

Ancient boxing appears to have been more dangerous and ferocious than its modern version. To have completed a career in the sport unwounded (*atraumatistos*), was a rare feat in itself. Few Greek boxers of the era could boast of such an accomplishment.

PANKRATION (MIXED COMBAT)

The brutal, bloody sport of pankration, or in the Latin spelling *pancratium*, was first introduced into the 33rd Olympiad in 648 B.C. The term is derived from the Greek adjectives *pan* and *kratos* and is translated to mean "all powers" or "all-encompassing." (The term itself has two distinct pronunciations: classic Greek dialect pronounced it "pag-raat-ee-oh"; it is expressed as "pan-cray-shun" in much of the modern world.) One who competed in such an event was referred to as a *pankratiast*.

Although it is not mentioned in writings prior to the 5th century B.C., there was a belief that pankration was founded by the great Attic hero Theseus, who combined his boxing and wrestling skills to defeat the fierce Minotaur in the labyrinth. Others credit the famed strongman and demigod Herakles (or Hercules in Latin) as its inventor. It would soon become the most spectacular and most demanding of all athletic events.

Pankration refers to an ancient combat sport based on martial technique and was essentially an all-out, no-holds-barred fight between two contestants. It integrated bare-knuckle boxing, kicking, and submission wrestling. Only biting and gouging were barred (but the tough Spartans allowed these, too, in their local sports festivals). This form of the sport became known as Spartan pankration. Victory was

The pankratiast on the left has seized an attempted kick to the stomach and prepares to throw his foe, who readies a chopping counterpunch to the head. (Greek vase, 490 B.C.)

Pankratiast delivering a low front kick. (Roman bronze figurine.)

sought with little or no regard for the danger to the body or life of one's opponent.

Some of the more popular pankration techniques included straight power punches, low kicks, elbowing and kneeing, arm locks and armbars, takedowns and throws, as well as numerous chokeholds. Another favored maneuver, known as *chancery*, involved grabbing an opponent by the hair and pulling him face-forward into an uppercutting fist or resounding knee strike. To many martial arts historians, pankration was in essence the "mixed martial arts" of classical Greece.

Kicking was an essential part of pankration, especially rising kicks to the stomach (*gastrizein*) and powerful sweeps meant to take an opponent off his feet. Kicks above the belt were used sparingly against a standing opponent, with blows aimed at the head or face only when one's adversary was on the ground and too weakened to block or catch the attacker's foot. Due to this unique tactic alone, many combative experts credit pankration as the first comprehensive unarmed fighting system on record.

There is no evidence of early pankratiasts' employing the stylized kicking methods seen in karate and tae kwon do today. In other words, there were no side kicks, back kicks, or spinning-type kicks. When kicks were used at all, they were usually in conjunction with a hand technique or as a distraction to get inside an opponent's defensive perimeter. From one Roman bronze, a pankratiast is depicted delivering a low kick with his heel to the opponent's knee. The obvious intent of the fighter is to break it. The frieze also displays perfect balance on the supporting foot with a lowering of his body weight as to deliver the attack with the body behind the blow. There also appears to be a simultaneous block and punching preparation. This is indicative of the high level of technique that the Greeks had developed in their native combat form, even at this time.

Striking in pankration was quite extensive and not limited to the closed fist. There are many images of fighters striking one another with a multitude of such hand weapons as with one's open palm or extended thumb, outstretched fingers, downward chops, and backfist blows. The prevalent striking tool, however, was a lunging straight punch to the head because much of the boxing was at long range. Although there is evidence from many existing frescoes of some infighting with hooks, uppercuts, and elbowing, most pankratiasts preferred to close with a grappling maneuver. This reflects another of pankration's principles: strike when fighting from a distance; grapple when you move inside.

Pankration bouts were extremely demanding and sometimes life-threatening to the competitors. Rules were few. As in all the heavy events, there were no weight divisions and no time limits. A referee (*hellanodikes*) was armed with a stout rod or switch to enforce the rules against biting and gouging. The rules, however, were often violated by some participants who, realizing they were outclassed by a heavier and stronger foe, would resort to such measures to escape being seriously maimed. A poet of the period dubbed one group of pankratiasts "the lions" because of their propensity for biting their

A Roman pankratiast traps his rival's hand and drives his knee into the groin. At right, a fighter wearing the lethal caestus *stands over his downed opponent. (Marble Roman relief, 2nd century B.C.)*

The "lunge."

Pankratiast punching and kicking his opponent simultaneously.

Pankratiasts gouging each other's eyes. The referee at right flogs them for this violation. (Greek vase, 480 B.C.)

opponents. The contest itself continued uninterrupted until one of the combatants either surrendered, suffered unconsciousness, or expired.

The fighting arena, or "ring," was no more than 12- to 14-feet square to encourage close-quarter action. The terrain on which the contestants waged combat was an area of soft, dug-up sand called a *skamma*. This *skamma* was obviously limiting to certain body maneuvers, such as rapid lateral movement, which contributed to the fact that size and strength became critical factors in pankration, as well as in the boxing and wrestling events.

In early accounts descriptions of pankration vary widely because it took differing forms according to individual preference and body stature. Any attempt, however, to classify it as either a ground-combat style or an "upright" method would be futile. By today's standards, ancient pankratiasts might be described as grapplers who freely used strikes to subdue their opposition. Others liken pankration to a kickboxing form with a heavy grappling influence.

There are stories of epic pankration matches that consisted solely of kicks and punches, with little or no wrestling moves employed. This form, referred to as *ano pankration*, required the combatants to remain standing and was considered a safer version of the sport. It was used more for training or preliminary bouts. The open style, *kato pankration*, was primarily used in the Games and was a much rougher form; the contest continued after the fighters went to the ground. It would be accurate to say that in the open style, the tall fighter with long reach relied primarily on hitting, whereas the shorter, thick-set man emphasized grappling. Either way,

pankration featured a diverse offensive arsenal, which proved appealing to Greece's top combat athletes.

Philostratus, a famous fight reporter in ancient Greece, wrote of pankratiasts:

> Pankratiasts practice a hazardous style of wrestling. They must employ falls backward, which are unsafe for the wrestler, and grips in which victory must be obtained by falling. They must possess skill in various methods of strangling; they also wrestle with an opponent's ankles, and twist his arm, besides hitting or jumping on him, for all these practices belong to the pankration, where only biting and gouging are prohibited. The Spartans allow even these practices, but the Eleans and the laws of the games exclude them, though they approve of strangulation.

Whereas biting requires no comment, Aristophanes describes the prohibited "gouging" as digging hands or fingers into an opponent's eyes, nose, mouth, or other tender body parts. Vividly illustrated in a vase painting, a pankratiast has inserted his thumb and finger into the opposing combatant's eye, and the official is hastening with an uplifted switch to punish this infraction of the rules. A similar scene appears in another illustration, where a pankratiast forces his hand into the mouth of his downed foe.

Fighters were paired off by drawing lots from a silver urn. The winners of each match fought each other until only two remained for the final bout. The winner of the event was always undefeated. Pankratiasts became proverbial for those

13

The pankratiast on top throttles his foe and pummels him into submission with his right fist. (Greek vase, 500 B.C.)

The top fighter has secured an armlock on his opponent and prevents him from escaping by trapping his leg with his own. (Greek bronze, Hellenistic era.)

athletes who were both physically and mentally prepared for all events. They assumed a stance that allowed good defense as well as attack. Their fingers were curled, midway between closing the fist and leaving the hand open, and in this manner they were quick to punch or grab as the situation demanded.

Pankratiasts usually began a match by sparring with their fists and open hands. Preliminary maneuvers, called *krocheirismos*, were employed at the onset and each fighter had his favorite opening technique. Sostratos of Sikyon was known as "Mr. Fingertips" (or the "fingerer")because he often tried to break his opponent's fingers at the beginning of a bout to secure an advantage. He was so successful with this trick that he won 12 crowns at Nemea and Corinth, three at Olympia, and two at Delphi.

Facing one another, each contestant attempted to bring the other heavily to the ground by grappling, hitting, kicking, or sweeping the legs. Another dramatic presentation of a pankration battle shows a fallen competitor bleeding profusely from the nose, while the markings of his opponent's blood-stained hands are visible on his back. His opponent has sprung upon him, grasping one arm with his left hand, and is preparing to finish him off with his cocked right fist.

Suffocation was not of the two-handed choking variety, but primarily employed the forearm across the windpipe or carotid artery. One favored technique was the *klimakismos* (ladder trick), a move in which a fighter got himself onto his opponent's back, encircled him with his legs, and constricted him from behind with his arms while simultaneously squeezing the abdomen with his legs. This tactic could be employed while both combatants were still on their feet or while they were grappling on the ground. The Eleans were particularly well known for their use of this technique, as well as other submission strangleholds.

A wrestler who was thrown to the ground was defeated, but a pankratiast might deliberately fall on his back (*hyptiasmos*) in order to throw his opponent more heavily or to gain a better strategic position. These types of techniques are common in judo and are often referred to as "sacrifice" maneuvers. One such tactic was the stomach throw, whereby the pankratiast seized his adversary by the shoulders or arms and fell backward, simultaneously planting his foot in his opponent's stomach to flip him forcefully over his head. The fighter who fell to the ground first was sometimes in a precarious position because his opponent would take advantage of the situation and attempt to mount him, immobilizing him with his legs, leaving his hands free to strike him or apply a stranglehold. The fighter on the bottom would attempt to turn on his back and employ his arms and legs to protect himself.

Locks applied to an opposing pankratiast's limbs were employed for the sole purpose of forcing one's foe into submission. Dislocated ankles, knees, and elbows were common injuries suffered during a match. Opportunities for applying joint-locking techniques were more frequent when one or both of the fighters were engaged in ground combat, where the contest was normally decided. As such, the struggle on the ground was often long and complicated, with the competitors sometimes sprawling full length, sometimes on top of one another, and sometimes on their knees. It was this aspect of pankration to which Plato, himself an Olympic wrestler, objected, and which compelled him to omit it from his ideal state as useless for warfare since "it did not teach men to keep their feet."

The aspiring pankratiast, along with the boxers, trained in the *korykeion*. In addition to the punch balls, there were larger sandbags, hung about 2 feet from the floor, for developing powerful low kicks, although some of the tougher disciples

Top fighter has obtained the mounted position by straddling his legs about his opponent's stomach. He is depicted snaking his arm under the throat to end the contest with a choke. (Roman clay lamp, 1st century B.C.)

The top pankratiast applying a painful double armlock in forcing the opposing fighter to submit. (Greek bronze, Hellenistic era.)

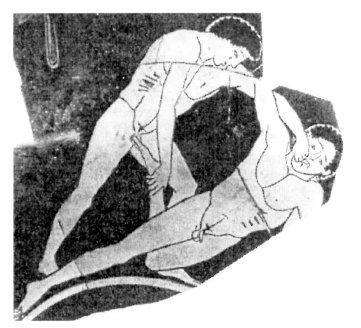

The standing pankratiast attempts to turn the opponent on his back by twisting the face and pulling his leg. (Greek vase, 500 B.C.)

were rumored to practice their leg techniques against tree trunks to toughen their feet and shins. Conditioning advocated stamina exercises such as running, stretching, and neck and abdominal work, as well as skiamachia to sharpen a fighter's movements and timing. In this drill, pankratiasts flailed the air with their strikes and kicks, similar to a modern boxer who throws his hand combinations in front of a mirror. Again, Antyllus describes this training as follows: "The shadowboxer must use not only his hands but also his legs, sometimes as if he were jumping, at other times as if he were kicking."

Pankration was taught progressively to students, who were usually divided into pairs for training. Once an appren-

tice fighter had learned the basic moves and combinations of the art, he would be permitted to engage in open sparring with other trainees. Sparring was emphasized to bring practice as close as possible to actual match conditions but with light contact to avoid being injured prior to a contest. A pankration trainer, according to the orator Quintillian, will not teach his pupil "only to strike with fist or foot, or merely instruct him in a few wrestling holds, but he will coach him in every department of that event."

Surprisingly, pankration was considered less dangerous than Greek boxing. While serious injuries and fatal accidents did sometimes occur, they were rare in comparison to those in boxing. Greek combat athletes who entered both events in a single Olympiad would fight in the pankration first, so as not to "spoil themselves" for boxing. This was not because pankration was less threatening. On the contrary, the problem was that those who competed in boxing would end up with bloody gashes on his body, and this would no doubt hamper their performance in pankration. On the other hand, a skilled pankratiast could survive the bare-handed contact without bloody wounds that would slow him down in the boxing bouts. Nonetheless, the punishment incurred in the all-out

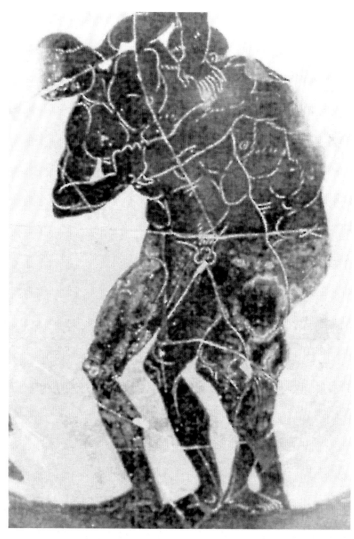

Pankratiast on the right grabs his opponent by the arms while attempting to sweep his feet from under him. (Greek vase, 480 B.C.)

Perhaps the most famous, though fatal, account was recorded by Philostratus during the early days of the sport. It describes renowned champion Arrichion of Phigaleia, who died and "won" at the same time. While being choked with the ladder trick, he twisted the challenger's ankle out of the socket with his last ounce of strength. The opponent raised his hand in submission as the winner expired.

The story of the Athenian Dioxippus is another striking example of a trained pankratiast's skill. During a drinking party in the camp of Alexander the Great, a Macedonian warrior by the name of Coragus challenged the Athenian, himself a pankration victor at Olympia in 336 B.C., to a duel. A day was appointed for the fight, and thousands of soldiers came to watch, each expecting a one-sided contest favoring their fellow soldier. The Macedonian was fully armed and armored while Dioxippus, as befitted a Greek athlete, stood naked and oiled and wielding only a club. Coragus first hurled a javelin, which Dioxippus dodged, and then jabbed with a spear, only to have his opponent smash it with his club. Finally, as Coragus reached for his dagger, Dioxippus grabbed Coragus' hand, forcing him off balance, and then swept his feet from under him. Dioxippus completed his conquest by placing his foot on his foe's throat while raising his club in a gesture of victory to the astounded onlookers.

There are many stories of the mythological Herakles. Legends agree that he killed the feared Nemean lion by strangling it, since its hide was impenetrable to strikes. Vase paintings show him executing a shoulder throw on the beast, as well as a standing headlock. Herakles also defeated Antaios (Latin: Anteus), the son of Earth (Gaia), who constantly drew sustenance from his mother during contests against his adversaries. According to Pindar, Antaios was an ogre who fought invited guests, killed them, and then buried their bodies in his palaistra. In their encounter, Herakles, although dwarfed by his much larger opponent, was able to kill Antaios simply by lifting him completely off the ground. This triumph marked the success of Hellenic skill over a savage who relied on magic for his strength.

Still another famed pankratiast, Polydamus of Scotussa in

combat matchup was such that the fighter who won both that contest and the boxing competition usually captured the latter event by *akoniti* (default) when his impressive showing in the pankration cowed the prospective boxers into withdrawing.

Some formidable fighters were able to excel in all three combative events. One such athlete, Cleitomachus of Thebes, was celebrated in an epigram after winning the triple victory at the Olympic games of 216 B.C.: "Immediately after taking off his blood-soaked gloves, he fought in the fierce pankration." This was after Cleitomachus had already defeated all comers in the wrestling event.

The exploits of the ancient pankratiasts became legendary in the annals of Greek athletics. Stories abound of past champions who were considered invincible beings, even to the extent that their feats rivaled those of the gods. Arrichion, Dioxippus, Herakles, and Polydamus are among the most recognized names, their accomplishments defying the odds by besting armed opponents in life-and-death combat, and battling and killing wild animals when human competition was no longer a challenge.

Pankratiast on top punches at his adversary's face in an attempt to escape from a tight headlock. (Greek vase, 500 B.C.)

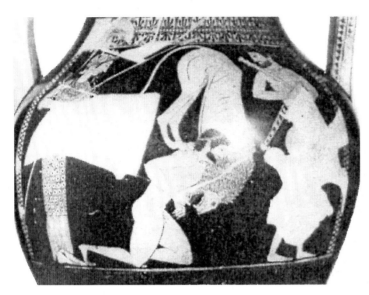

Herakles throwing the Nemean lion over his shoulder. (Greek vase, 530–515 B.C.)

Herakles trips Antaios backward by lifting his ankle out from under him and bringing the fight to the ground. (Greek vase, 515–500 B.C.)

Thessaly, was known to have fought and killed three of the Immortals, bodyguards to Persian kings, who had invited the champion athlete to Susa to exhibit his skill. In what was supposed to be a friendly match, Polydamus' opponents attempted to defeat him at the same time, only to meet their deaths.

Exhibitions of superhuman strength were common, with boxers and pankratiasts often smashing stones and planks with their bare fists and driving their hardened feet through bronze war shields. There are references in Greek myths to a fire that, when it burns brightly enough in the depths of a man's soul, makes him almost godlike in his abilities. This internal energy was called *arete* and was thought to be the essence of a champion pankratiast's extraordinary skill.

Pankration continued to be practiced until the early centuries of the Christian era, but already during the Hellenistic period, when Greece had lost its independence, certain negative elements caused the decline of the sport. This was due in part to its more violent characteristics, but principally because of the takeover by professionalism. An excess of purses and honors to the athletic champions of all Greek sports had brought about social complications. The corruption inherent in professional athletics were considered worse in boxing, wrestling, and pankration, in particular. This "evil" was increased by the absence of weight divisions, which made these contests the monopoly of the heavyweight athlete. Consequently, the matches became less scientific and even more brutal.

The greatest military leaders of ancient Greece had disapproved of combat sports and pankration in particular, frequently criticizing it because of its emphasis on groundwork and sacrifice-type moves. Nonetheless martial-art skills, including those used in pankration, were a significant force in military training. Historical accounts of Sparta with its great battle at Thermopylae against the Persians attest to the weaponless fighting skills of the trained soldier. Even grossly outnumbered, the Greeks had fought tenaciously with sword, spear, and shield, and those who were disarmed continued, gouging eyes, kicking through leg armor, and throwing their opponents to the hard ground.

Pankration was basic to the majority of the Greek *hoplites* who served under Alexander the Great during his invasion of India in the 4th century B.C. Many authorities now contend that this dispersal of pankration techniques throughout the subcontinent laid the foundation for the countless Asian martial arts that evolved soon thereafter, including Chinese kung fu, Okinawan karate, and Japanese jujutsu. The subject has been one of controversy and conjecture for many years. In the West, it was always accepted that the Greek fighting arts spawned the sports of boxing and wrestling as we know them today.

Perhaps the demise of ancient pankration was also due to the lack of an underlying philosophy strong enough to prevent it from becoming a mere spectacle as opposed to a true art form. What resulted was a gradual loss of the old ideals of *aidos* inspired by the Greeks. What had begun as an essential part of a warrior's training and flourished as a challenging sport wound up a corrupt and discredited form of prizefighting. Even so, pankration never completely vanished. Variations would appear from time to time in Greece, but they were pale shadows of the original form, with the fighters dressed in trunks, and with the addition of groin strikes to the list of enjoined techniques. Its popularity, especially in the 19th and 20th centuries, would take a backseat to wrestling, which the Greeks considered a much safer sport. It is accurate to say that Greco-Roman wrestling survives as a legacy of these classic combat sports.

One cannot, however, deny the significance of pankration as a comprehensive martial art of antiquity. It was, in fact, an almost limitless system, its broad spectrum of techniques bridging the gap between striking and grappling. As such, pankration reigns as the preeminent combative method of the ancient world.

HISTORY OF HELLENIC MARTIAL ARTS

Jim Arvanitis' extraordinary flexibility is shown in this high kick.

THE EVOLUTION OF MODERN PANKRATION

In the process of development and improvement, many martial arts styles and derivations have evolved from the old. After years of intense training and investigation, the best carefully selected fighting techniques were extracted and modified into a single system. Added to this were modern training methodology and principles of kinesiology (body mechanics). But the concepts of the classic art remained the main ingredient, actually the thread that held this mix together. This, in essence, was the birth of modern pankration and *μ (mu) τ (tau)* or Greek martial art in the early 1970s. The Greek symbols, *mu tau*, are an acronym for *mahitiki tehni*, the Greek term for *martial art*. Modern pankration is the sports component of mu tau. The following elements make up its foundation.

FORMS OF MODERN PANKRATION

- Sport pankration (limited-rules combat competition)
- Spartan pankration (NHB combat geared to the street)

MODERN PANKRATION TECHNICAL ELEMENTS

- Punching, striking, and elbowing techniques
- Kicking and kneeing techniques
- Takedowns, throws, and sweeping techniques
- Submission holds and joint-locking techniques
- Submission chokes and strangulation techniques

MODERN PANKRATION TRAINING METHODOLOGY

- Endurance training
- Strength training
- Striking-tool development training
- Skills application training
- Sparring

MODERN PANKRATION CHARACTERISTICS

- **Fluid readiness position.** Emphasis is on a well-braced stance that allows for elusive motion and is adaptable to either boxing, kicking, or grappling techniques.
- **Motion economy in defense and attack.** There is no wasted time or movement. Offensive tools, parries, evasions, and blocks are executed with minimal effort and turn defense into instantaneous attack.
- **Ranges of combat.** There are three basic combat ranges: long (kicking), medium (punching), and infighting, where elbows, knees, and grappling techniques are employed. Offense is not limited by stylized preferences but is *total*. The practitioner is equally skillful as a boxer, kicker, or grappler. He poses a danger from any distance, unlike some stylists who favor hands over feet or prefer to fight at long range from their adversaries.
- **No high kicks.** Greek martial art emphasized low-line kicks for use on the battlefield and in the arena. These techniques are "safer" to execute than high kicks, which tend to leave you off balance and vulnerable to attack. Kicks to the face or head from an upright position are reserved more for training than for actual combat.
- **Heavy use of training equipment.** The palaistra offers striking shields, heavy bags, focus gloves, double-end speed bags, safety padding, and headgear because such equipment allows for more realistic practice, as well as bet-

ter power and speed development. This equipment enables practitioners of this fighting art to strike with full force against a moving target.

- **Focus on suddenly closing the gap.** One of the key elements in sport pankration is to spot an opening and immediately close the distance to make the transition to infighting range. From here a clinch ensues, followed by a takedown to force the action to the ground. In this position, pure "stand-up" fighters will be unfamiliar with the combat conditions because their punches and kicks are rendered useless.

- **Emphasis on grappling skills in close.** Although punches, kicks, and strikes have their place in combat, it is inevitable that fights often end up on the ground. This is the level where grappling techniques prove effective. It is our contention that punching and kicking skills are *not* enough for the conditions of the street.

- **Functional attack tools.** Combat techniques must be simple and efficient. There is no time for flashy, complicated moves, such as spinning kicks or flowery hand movements. Perfect form is secondary to causing maximum damage and resolving the conflict swiftly.

- **Reality training.** Street practicality is underscored in Greek martial art. Training is geared to simulate actual fight conditions as closely as possible. It does not waste time on unrealistic, prearranged patterns or forms (i.e., kata). Sparring with full contact and protective gear is the ultimate learning experience. Emphasis is on adaptability rather than memorized response to deal with the unpredictability of real combat.

- **Spartan conditioning.** Conditioning exercises to develop strength and endurance have long been stressed in the pankratiast's development. Weight resistance training, rope jumping, and distance running are included to equip the practitioner with the physical attributes necessary to outlast and overcome the opposition.

Pankration is indeed Western martial arts. Unlike a conventional Asian style with its emphasis on prearranged drilling (e.g., kata, one-step sparring), a technique's utility is determined ultimately through full-contact sparring, simulating realistic combat conditions. All of its teachings are geared to this end, free of the superfluous and the nonessentials, and streamlined into the purely functional. The pankratiast is one who never meets a situation according to a predicted pattern but reacts spontaneously, improvising his approach and tactics according to the uncertain actions presented by his opponent.

Although contemporary in many ways, modern pankration preserves the Greek tradition of athleticism. It emphasizes that a martial art is first and foremost an athletic endeavor and not some mystical experience that gives one devastating powers. Pankration also stresses the importance of realism in training. To learn fighting requires that you fight and become cognizant of all those aspects that make up a real fight. Admittedly, even a street fight cannot be completely duplicated in any martial art because of its unpredictability; Hellenic combat sport has always attempted to simulate it as closely as possible.

One must also learn to wage combat on the ground. This is certainly where many outcomes of real fights are decided, and the practitioner must be well versed in grappling to overcome his opponent from this position. Upright styles that emphasize kicking and punching are useless on the ground if they are not schooled in ground tactics. A proficient grappler can easily get inside a foe's arms and legs and wrestle him down. This has been proven over and over again, from the ancient Panhellenic games to the limited-rules combat events of today.

Mu tau is a distinct art—the expression of oneself in combat. It is not a style: styles tend to dissect what was once whole into preferential parts. Some favor hands over feet, striking over grappling; and some are very spectacular. Yet none of these styles offers a complete fighting system in itself. The goal of mu tau, as inspired by the ancient Greeks, is to be well rounded. The pankratiast is trained to be effective in either an upright posture or on the ground, against single or multiple opponents, and in both unarmed and armed situations. In a one-on-one struggle, grappling and going to the ground might be the main strategy. However, against more than one opponent or in facing a weapon, the striking aspect and remaining on one's feet may be favored. Everything depends on the circumstances, and the pankratiast adapts accordingly.

In summary, then, mu tau is a modern Greek martial art embracing pankration as its nucleus. It might be described as an exclusive combat system, a Westernized martial arts hybrid whose theme is total fighting freedom. Not merely a blending of techniques, this system preserves a history and philosophy of ancient Greek tradition. And while it may be physically very similar to other styles, it has a unique conceptual base in ancient Hellenic civilization, fusing skill, discipline, and Spartan honor to a way of life. For this reason alone, mu tau stands as the first modern form of Hellenic martial art of its kind.

CHAPTER 3

BASIC ANO COMBAT SKILLS

Stand-up fighting is referred to in Greek as *ano pankration*. This important "level" consists of the following elements: the ready position, footwork, distancing, angling, offensive strikes and kicks, upright grappling, and defenses. This chapter examines each of these areas with the exception of standing grappling techniques, which are discussed separately in Chapter 5.

READINESS POSITION
(*THESI MACHIS*)

The basic premise in sport pankration is that all fights commence from an upright position but frequently end on the ground. The readiness position then can be defined as the starting point for all defense and attack. Referred to in Greek as *thesi machis*, it is a stand-up pose made up of the on-guard and the stance. The on-guard refers to the placement of the arms and hands, while the stance is the positioning of the feet and trunk.

The stance features an upright posture with the feet placed slightly more than shoulder-width apart. If the fighter is right-handed, he places his right hand and foot in front, which is referred to as the *southpaw* position. With the left hand and foot forward, the fighter assumes the *orthodox* position, where the front foot is flat on the ground with the rear foot poised on the ball of the foot, keeping the heel elevated to about 3 inches to promote quick, springy movement. The knees are always slightly bent with weight equally distributed on both legs. A well-balanced but mobile stance is the main characteristic of a modern pankratiast's ready pose.

Jim Arvanitis and sparmate exchanging kicks.

21

The torso should be turned sideways in most cases, with the lead shoulder facing the opponent. By angling in this manner, the pankratiast protects the midsection and adds greater reach to the lead striking weapons. The chin is tucked into the chest for protection, and the eyes are on the opponent at all times, looking into his upper chest. This enables you to detect any movement executed with either hands or feet.

The placement of the feet is transitory, depending on the actual technique that is executed. For example, when punching, the modern pankratiast assumes the *parathesis* position, which is more of a boxing stance, with the torso angled more toward the opponent. In round kicking, which is the dominant kicking tool, the body more squarely faces the adversary in what is referred to as the *systasis* stance. This allows for a quicker and more powerful delivery of the kicking leg. Once the grappling range is entered, the position of the feet may be altered again by lowering the center of gravity to gain more leverage to apply forceful takedowns and other maneuvers.

The fists should be held at about chin height. A common error is to drop the lead arm, leaving the entire midsection and head exposed. Just as dangerous is holding both hands below chin level. The upper body leans slightly forward at the waist (not the shoulders) to help cover and tighten the abdominal muscles. In addition to body protection, tilting forward brings you closer to your opponent, which enhances your power, reach, leverage, and accuracy in punching.

These upper-body positioning concepts are much more effective than standing militarily erect with the head up and back straight all the time. Such a position often finds the fighter backing away from blows rather than holding his ground and retaliating. Staying within striking range is essential to the pankratiast's offensive efficiency.

FOOTWORK

A modern pankratiast's footwork is best described as light, loose, and "springy." A fighter should never move flat-footed, but should be up slightly on the balls of his feet, alert and ready to shift direction in a split second. Movement must be smooth and economical. Quick, nimble footwork is essential to successful scoring of one's kicks and punches, as well as moving in quickly to execute takedowns. If one's footwork is slow, the tools will be hard-pressed to accomplish their objective.

Good footwork is stressed and is used for three purposes:

- **Defensive footwork.** To present an elusive target for the opponent, one that is extremely difficult to hit or grab hold of. For example, lateral movement takes the body out of the direct line of attack.
- **Offensive footwork.** To move in on the opponent, to suddenly and explosively bridge the gap (i.e., close the distance) to execute one's attacks.
- **Strategic footwork.** To move around the opponent, searching for openings while maintaining a distance where you are safe and he is not.

DISTANCING

Distancing, or the spatial relationship between combatants, is critical to any fighter. In modern pankration, we recognize two distinct ranges: striking and grappling. The striking range is for upright fighting and is broken down further into long, medium, and infighting. Each range is considered equally important, and the fighter must be able to cope with the conditions presented at both of these distances and turn them to his advantage.

Southpaw position (front view).   *Southpaw position (side view).*   *Orthodox position (front view).*   *Orthodox position (side view).*

STRIKING RANGE

Long Range

Perhaps the safest upright striking range is the long range. This distance enables the pankratiast to deliver kicking techniques with his longest weapons, his legs. At this distance, the major function of the hands is for either deception or defense. This range is not considered the primary fighting distance in pankration.

Medium Range

Next is the medium range, in which boxing techniques play a dominant offensive role. Straight-line blows, such as the lunging jab, the Spartan spear, and reverse thrust, are employed from this range.

Infighting Range

The third and final upright striking range is infighting. This position features the more compact punching techniques, such as hooks and uppercuts, in addition to neck grabs, and lethal elbow and knee strikes.

GRAPPLING RANGE

The grappling range is sometimes the dominant fighting distance in sport pankration. Once the fighters have closed the gap and go into a clinch, the action almost always goes to the ground where the strategy of the trained pankratiast is to end the conflict.

ANGLING

Angling refers to the exact strategic location from which to execute an attack or defend against oncoming blows or head-down charges. Greek combat recognizes three specific angles, each determined by the body positioning of both fighters. A skillful pankratiast always attempts to find his opponent's weaknesses while avoiding his strengths. The proper angle depends to a great degree on the stances employed by the combatants. Each man tries to offset his foe's timing and sense of rhythm by constantly varying his positional angles.

UPRIGHT STRATEGIC ANGLES

Direct Angulation
The fighter, regardless of stance, is positioned in front of the opponent.

Direct angling.

Outside Angulation
The southpaw fighter positions himself to his *left* of the opposing right-stancer and to his *right* of the orthodox stancer.

The orthodox fighter positions himself to his *right* of the opposing left-stancer and to his *left* of the southpaw stancer.

Outside angling.

Inside Angulation
The southpaw fighter positions himself to his *right* of the opposing right-stancer and to his *left* of the orthodox stancer.

The orthodox fighter positions himself to his *left* of the opposing left-stancer and to his *right* of the southpaw stancer.

Inside angling.

Rear Flank

This positioning is the perfect placement from which to attack one's adversary and is referred to as "attacking the blind side." A wide assortment of strikes, takedowns, and finishing holds can be administered from this position, either while standing or on the ground.

Rear flank.

STRIKING TOOLS

Pankration striking techniques are made up of any blow with the open hand, closed fist, elbow, foot, shin, or knee. These blows are applicable from either an upright posture or when both fighters are struggling on the ground, and they consist of punching, gouging, elbowing, kicking, and kneeing.

The hands are the major close-range striking tools. Of these techniques, there are four basic punches, each having specific advantages in terms of angles and distances. Some punches are classified as minor blows: that is, while they are not ordinarily designed to inflict severe damage on an opponent, they set up a major or knockout blow or follow-up grappling maneuver.

HAND TECHNIQUES

The Lead Jab

The lead jab is perhaps the most important hand tool in sport pankration. It is a straight-line blow aimed primarily at the opponent's face. It is used as the initial strike or feint in almost every punching flurry, and it closes the distance for the harder blows as well as grappling takedowns. It is also used for stopping an oncoming attack. The jab is delivered with the forward hand and makes a quarter-turn to land on its target horizontally. Attempting to land jabs to the body is rare because bending forward to hit this area increases the risk of running into a counterpunch or elbow strike.

The jab can be delivered while the fighter remains well covered by the rear hand. This is important in case a blow misses its mark. It is often wise to deliver multiple jabs because the second or third one has a chance of landing even after the first has missed. Sustained jabbing keeps the opposing fighter on the defensive and constantly off balance.

Two types of jabs are used: a quick, snappy strike with quick retraction and a stiff jab that carries greater body force and follow-through. Both blows are delivered with a "lunge," a long, quick step or shuffle forward from medium range.

A lead jab with a lunge step.

Lead jab to the face.

The simple body mechanics and quickness of the Spartan spear enable the fighter to maintain good balance at all times. As a result, it is often used for a sustained assault and for setting up other techniques. Though not part of Olympic or sport pankration, eye attacks were commonly employed in the deadly, anything-goes Spartan style.

Spartan spear to the opponent's eye.

Spartan Spear

This hand technique is much like the lead jab punch but with the fingers extended. The sole target is the eyes and is designed to incapacitate the opponent by blinding him. The use of the finger strike as a serious self-defense weapon abides by the old Greek adage that "if one cannot see you, he cannot hit you." The blow employs the front hand, with the first three fingers curled into a point and the thumb held in. Speed and accuracy, not power, are the essential elements in this attack. With the shorter distance it has to travel to reach its mark and the added 3 or 4 inches in reach, the spear is considered a highly efficient tool in the modern pankratiast's offensive arsenal.

Reverse Thrust

Also called the rear cross, this hand tool is classified as a power punch in pankration. It is a straight-line punch using the rear hand and is delivered chiefly to the head in the form of a counter, as a follow-up to a feint, or as the finishing stroke in a punching combination.

The technique derives considerable power from the greater distance it has to travel to its target and the fact that you have the full weight of the body behind the blow. Power comes from a swivel of the hips and a pivot on the ball of the back foot. The punching fist makes a quarter-turn in its delivery and lands horizontally on its mark. The leading hand protects by folding back by the chin to cover and deflect return punches if necessary.

Spartan spear.

Reverse thrust.

Rear thrust to the opponent's face.

Hook Punch

The hook is a short, crushing blow that travels outside the opponent's line of vision in a circular motion to attack the chin, side of the head, solar plexus, or ribs. Primarily an inside-range tool, the hook is employed as a strong counter or follow-up blow, which often catches an opponent moving in. In extremely close quarters, the hook can also function as an effective lead when an adversary sports an airtight guard that cannot be penetrated by straight-line blows. Usually, the hook follows other maneuvers, such as a feint or lead jab, to obtain the best leverage.

The hook is never a wide, looping movement, but rather a compact blow, one that travels no more than 8 to 10 inches. Power is supplied by getting the shoulder and hips into the punch. The hand should not telegraph that it is on the way by withdrawing, winding up, or dropping before delivery. The body simply turns away from the arm until the play of the shoulder joint is used to the limit.

The secret to powerful hooking is leverage—shifting the weight of the body behind the blow at the exact moment of impact. Maximum body weight is transmitted into the punch, with the arm serving as the conductor of the force. Potent hooks are *not* arm punches; they are the result of maximizing one's own body weight into the attack.

High lead hook.

Lead hook to the opponent's jaw.

27

Low lead hook.

Lead hook to the head.

Lead hook to the opponent's solar plexus.

High rear hook.

Low rear hook.

Rear hook to the jaw of the opponent.

Rear hook to the opponent's body.

Lead uppercut to the chin. *Lead uppercut to the body.* *Rear uppercut.*

Either hand can be used in hooking, although the lead is favored. Most hook punches are also directed to the head. The lead hook to the body is executed by bending the front knee so that the shoulder is on line with the target. The rear hand is positioned high to shield the face, and the elbow is held tight to the body to protect the ribs. The chin should be positioned behind the lead shoulder to avoid being tagged by a rear cross counter or elbow attack. All the weight is over the front foot as the fighter pivots into the blow. The hand "digs" at an angle into the ribs or solar plexus.

The rear hook is very similar in delivery to the lead hook except that the puncher twists his back foot to gain power. The rear heel lifts as the weight of the body is transferred to the front leg. The rear hook is primarily a head shot, although it is sometimes used to the body.

Lead uppercut to the opponent's chin.

Uppercut

Like the hook, the uppercut is a potent close-range punching tool. It is best used against an opponent who moves in close with head-down charges or who favors crouching and staying low in his on-guard position. This technique is not very useful against the upright fighter, who prefers jabbing and kicking from a relatively safe distance. Actually, the uppercut is a form of the hook except that it is delivered upward instead of from the side. It features a scooping motion with your palm toward you and can be administered with either hand. The targets are the point of the jaw, the face, the ribs, and the solar plexus.

Lead uppercut to the opponent's solar plexus.

CHANCERY

An ancient technique very popular when using the uppercut is chancery. This involves pulling the opponent's hair and jerking him face forward into an uppercutting fist. The blow is delivered to either the chin or body.

Hairpull and uppercut to the chin.

Hairpull and uppercut to the solar plexus.

ELBOW STRIKES

The elbow strike (*agkohnizein*) is one of the most powerful and dangerous weapons in close-quarter stand-up combat. In modern pankration there are two basic techniques using the elbow for stand-up fighting: forward strike and downward strike. The downward elbow is also employed as a ground-striking tactic when the pankratiast has attained a position of controlling the opponent from being on top.

Elbow strikes are performed following the same theoretical principles as hand techniques. Power is generated

Lead elbow strike.

Rear elbow strike.

by rotating the entire body behind the attack. They are never the starting blow in an attack but usually are the second or third strike in a series. They frequently follow a lead jab. They are also effectively used as counters. The primary targets are the head and base of the neck. When toe-to-toe or from a clinch where the arms are trapped, the elbows can be freely utilized.

Elbow strikes should be practiced whereby the right elbow strike immediately follows the left elbow strike and vice versa. These techniques are frequently executed by stepping forward slightly.

An elbow attack is difficult to defend against because of the close range and speed. The most common defenses include full-cover and forearm blocks.

Rear elbow to face.

Downward elbow.

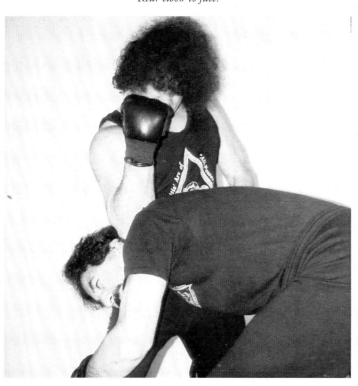

Down elbow to the neck.

31

KICKING TECHNIQUES

Pankration was one of the first, if not the first, to have included kicking techniques (*laktisma*) in its extensive arsenal of offensive tools. Evidence points to the fact that many of early pankration's kicks were aimed low to the lower stomach and legs. Writings of the early Greek fight reporters also indicate the use of both the direct, or front, and round kicking movements. The latter technique was a favored means of sweeping the legs from under an opponent and bringing combat to the ground where grappling and hitting were employed together so effectively by the Greek champions.

Further documentation also shows that the later adoption of pankration by Greek military units brought about new foot attack tools, such as an angular kick delivered very similarly to the side kick seen in many modern karate styles as well as in French savate. Legend has it that some highly skilled hoplites used this kick in battle to penetrate the shields wielded by their enemies. In many museums around the world, there are vase paintings depicting Greek fighters kneeing and stomping on a downed combatant during a contest.

The martial arts contain a number of flashy, complicated kicking maneuvers, such as spinning and flying techniques and multiple kicking with the same leg. In pankration, such moves are never used because they lack the accuracy and power to wear down and damage the opponent. These kicks may certainly look impressive, but more often than not they leave you off balance and more vulnerable to being countered. They are more suited to a tournament or controlled environment than the serious conditions of a street brawl.

Although kicks are the primary long-range artillery, they are not considered a major offense, as they are in many Korean and Chinese martial arts styles. For the most part, kicking in pankration serves as a prelude to, or is used in conjunction with, a hand technique. As with other striking techniques, kicks are also employed as a distraction to set the opponent up for a takedown.

Modern pankration's kicking weapons consist of the shod foot, shin, and knee. In using the foot, proper positioning in the various kicks is critical. Kicks lack their full destructive force if the foot is not properly positioned. Proper foot positions absorb the shock of impact, preventing such injuries as broken toes or ankle sprains. The six weapons employed in modern pankration kicking techniques are as follows:

- **Toe (point of shoe).** Formed by curling the toes down, the toe is used for lead- and back-leg round kicks at longer range.
- **Heel.** Formed by pulling the foot straight back, this weapon is used exclusively in the low side kick.
- **Instep.** Formed by curling the tip of the shod foot down, the instep is used in lead- and back-leg round kicks from longer range.
- **Ball of foot.** The foot is kept straight with the toes pulled back tightly and used exclusively when executing front thrust kicks.

- **Shin.** The shin is the lower part of the leg used in round kicking techniques executed from closer range. Mu tau pankratiasts toughen this area to a great degree by kicking heavy bags repeatedly in training.
- **Knee.** The knee is used for close-range combat; either the front or side of the knee can be used.

Attacking the legs is emphasized in modern pankration. Leg kicks are both powerful and difficult to defend against. With a single successful attack, all the opponent's faculties—offense, defense, mobility—are simultaneously impaired.

Leg kicks are usually used as first-stage attacks. They can lead into more complex offensives, they can be employed to "feel out" an adversary, or they can keep an opposing fighter at a distance momentarily, gaining you time and space for the next stage of attack. Whether it is part of a more complex strategy or not, a well-placed, full-powered leg attack can take down or disable even the best combatant.

The opponent's front leg is the primary target for low kicks. As it is nearest to you, it is the easiest to reach, as well as the slowest to leave, striking range. The best time to attack an opponent's front leg is when he is either stationary or advancing, since he will find it difficult to avoid the blow and his own forward momentum may contribute to the impact. Areas of the leg to be attacked are the shin, knee, back of the knee, calf, and thigh. The downward side kick and both the lead- and back-leg roundhouse kicks are chiefly used in mu tau pankration leg attacks.

Of the six kicking tools, the most functional are those directed toward the lower body with a short, fast trajectory. It is a common tactic of pankratiasts to always try the simplest, most reliable techniques first and to go on to the more complicated ones only if the simpler ones do not work.

Front Snap Kick to Groin

Pankratiasts have long used this foot attack for combat. The application of this kicking tool is very much like that of the lead-jab punch. It can be used as a finishing kick, as the kick for creating openings, or in a series of hand and foot techniques. And like the jab, it uses the lead limb. There is no "chambering" to this technique, whereby the knee is raised high into the chest area prior to delivery. After sliding in with the rear foot, the front leg snaps from the lower leg at the opponent's groin area. The tip of the shoe is the striking point.

Front Thrust Kick

The front thrust kick is similar to the front groin kick, except with more power. A slight chambering motion is employed in this technique, enabling the hips to drive forward for greater penetrating force. The ball of the foot is used primarily to attack the lower stomach or in some cases the kneecap. When delivered to the body, it is used more as a push to keep the opposing fighter at a distance. This is a favored kick to stop the opponent's back-leg round kick.

Front snap kick to the groin.

Front thrust kick to the lower stomach.

Front thrust kick to the solar plexus.

Front thrust kick to the opponent's knee.

33

Hook Kick

The hook kick is delivered with the lead leg on a medium or low line with the point of the shoe extended. Its delivery features a short, outward step for greater hip rotation in the blow.

Readiness positions. Pankratiast on the right assumes the southpaw stance.

Lead hook kick to the thigh.

Footwork in the maneuver involves crossing the left foot in front of the lead foot by stepping outward and pivoting on the supporting foot. The lead leg is chambered slightly.

The supporting leg should be kept straight for medium hook kicks and bent for low hook kicks. The knee faces the target with the foot extended along the cocked leg. The targets vary: ribs, solar plexus, stomach, and kidneys for medium-line hook kicks; the thighs for low hook kicks. The thigh kick is a very common attack in pankration. As in any kick, the head can be attacked with the foot if the opposing fighter is on the ground and clearly vulnerable.

Round Kick

In contrast to the hook kick, the round kick uses the back leg, with the body pivoting on the ball of the rear foot. Sometimes, an outward step precedes the pivoting motion, which enhances the kicking force. In executing this technique, the kicking foot starts from a stance with the body more squared to the opponent. With the arms and hands protecting the head and torso, the body pivots on the ball of the front foot with a simultaneous rotation of the hips. The kicking leg goes immediately to its intended target in an arc, with no

Kick lands on the outside of the thigh as the kicker completes a pivot on the ball of the supporting foot.

chambering motion. The object is to fully turn into the kick and follow through with maximum penetration. This technique is more similar to the one in Thai boxing than that in karate or tae kwon do, which emphasizes an initial chambering action. It is delivered with the swing of the entire body, and not only with a snap of the lower leg. The instep or shin is used as the striking surface, depending on the distance, and the targets include the thigh and body.

Round kick to the thigh.

Round kick against a punch.

Execution of Low Round Kick

1

Readiness positions. The pankratiast on the left assumes an orthodox stance.

2

The pankratiast on the left pivots on the ball of his supporting front foot and swings his whole body behind his right leg. There is no leg chambering.

3

The kick lands on the outside of the thigh with full follow-through of the turning body.

35

Back-leg round kick to the opponent's body

Side kick to the knee.

Back-leg round kick to the head of the opponent on the ground.

Side Kick

This powerful foot weapon is used as a full-powered thrust rather than a snap. It is delivered solely to the low line. The side kick is a quick and ravaging low-line stamp designed to dislocate or snap an opponent's leg with a single well-placed blow. Best used with the slide footwork from the on guard, the lead leg is thrust straight out and down at the shin or kneecap in one fluid motion. A useful prelude to the move is a distracting upward feint with the forward hand. Contact is

Downward side kick to the opponent's knee.

made with the bottom of the foot or heel. Due to the potential force of this kick, the outside foot edge or blade is not used, since a broken foot could easily result.

Offensively, the downward side kick is almost impossible to block. In the street, the average brawler would not expect it and has no adequate defense against it. Logically, it is the best offense to apply at the onset of a fight. The shin and knee are the targets located closest to you, and because they are exposed they are difficult to protect. Also, the downward side kick is a good means of bridging the gap to employ combinations.

Defensively, this kick can be used to stop almost any kind of oncoming strike or kick. The concept of the defensive application is to beat your adversary's timing with your superior leg reach: you must attempt to intercept your opponent while he is in motion and fully committed, just before or during the moment he is launching his blow. The downward side kick is highly effective for this purpose because it uses the longest weapon to the nearest open target.

The downward side kick is not only a very powerful kick but is also a relatively safe tool to employ. Since the side of your body faces the opponent throughout the maneuver, very few of your most vital targets are ever exposed to his attack. The kick also offers a secure distance outside the opponent's fist range.

Knee kick to solar plexus.

Side kick to the shin against a jab to the face.

Knee kick to the face.

Knee Kick

The use of the knee (*gonato*) provides the combatant with a dangerous infighting weapon. There are two types of knee kicks employed instinctively by fighters once they clinch or are able to grab each other about the neck: front and round. The primary targets are the contained head and body and the part of the leg above the knee.

Once a firm grasp about the neck is secured, the pankra-

BASIC ANO COMBAT SKILLS

Knee kick to the opponent's ribs.

tiast has been trained to unleash a series of devastating knee attacks, with either the lead leg or back leg, into his opposition. Surviving such an onslaught requires not only the highest level of skill but also superb physical fitness. Knee strikes are delivered with the lower leg pulled back, toes pointed down, and upper body leaning away at a 45-degree angle. Following these principles provides protection against head shots while employing knee strikes in close.

Neck clinch.

1

Neck clinch.

2

Knee kick to the solar plexus.

Knee kick to the opponent's thigh with a waist clinch.

Applying a neck clinch (*hamma*) is an integral part of an effective knee attack. Clinching allows the fighter to control his adversary while keeping him close enough for the knee to land solidly and accurately. It is important that from this close range the pankratiast's head is never dropped because this will open the face up to the opponent's knee technique. The fighter must also keep the elbows close together. The hands are crossed high on the opponent's head, and the forearms are used for leverage to pull him forward into the knee.

The knee can also be employed to attack the leg area at the thigh. Rather than grabbing the neck, however, the pankratiast is trained to clinch the opposing fighter about the waist when applying this technique.

KEY POINTS IN STRIKING/
KICKING EXECUTION

- For speed and accuracy, all striking techniques must be executed from the ready position without winding up, so as to avoid telegraphing the intended action.
- After completing a punch or kick, the striking limb must be immediately retracted to the ready or on-guard placement.
- The shoulders and arms must be kept loose and relaxed when hitting; the muscles of the body contract only at the moment of impact.
- It is important to get leverage into every blow for maximum power. Effective punching and kicking is the result of using the entire body in the blow, not arm or leg strength alone.
- The rear or guarding hand is always positioned to protect the upper body from a counter. The rear hand does most of the defensive work and supplements the other hand. If one hand is hitting, the other should be protecting the body. It is always in position, correlating to the uncovered line or unprotected area. And it is always tactically placed for an offensive follow-up.
- The rear hand is also used offensively but more as a counter or as part of a combination (following a lead jab, for example). More power is generated than with the forward hand because of the added distance and the fact that the full use of the body is employed behind the punch.
- Punching is practiced with economy of motion and accuracy, and from a variety of angles, both as single blows and as combinations. The goal is to be able to deliver blows in fluid series and to ultimately synchronize the punching techniques with all other attack tools.
- The pankratiast must be careful not to initiate power blows, such as hook punching and elbow and knee strikes, from too far out because it will make him vulnerable to counteroffensives.
- For maximum force and penetration, kicks should always be delivered with the upper body leaning slightly forward into the attack. The body should not lean back and upset the fighter's balance and nullify the potential for follow-ups.
- The arms should be guarding the head and body during all kicks and be instantly ready to be used in the offensive.
- Avoid these common errors in delivering jabs and hooks: lifting the rear foot off the ground, dropping the front shoulder, lowering the rear guard, or dropping the front hand after punching to create an opening.

DEFENSES

Although pankration has long been attack oriented, a protective defense cannot be overlooked. Taking the tough-guy attitude of "I'll take a shot to give one" is *not* a very wise tactic and only serves to take its toll on a fighter. Coming away from a fight the victor but still bloodied and hurt is the strategy of the poorly schooled combatant. Effective defensive skills were lacking in the earliest form of pankration, but through time and with modification they have been developed to a high degree in its descendant art.

The following are the basic stand-up defensive techniques that are critical to the modern pankratiast's survival in upright fighting. It is essential to bear in mind that a fighter cannot begin to possess a potent offense until he has first mastered an airtight defense.

Arm and Leg Blocks

The pankratiast is trained to maintain a tight guard with the hands close together at chin height and the elbows held close to the rib cage. From this position, the fighter should be able to block a high percentage of the opponent's punches and elbow blows by taking them on the arms. Against close-range hooks, the defender should cover with his rear arm. For defending against a power round kick, a raised knee against

Rear arm block against a hook to the head.

Full cover against an elbow to the head.

the shin or a straight knee angled inward to the inner thigh as the kick is delivered is the best defense. These function as effective counters as well.

Since low kicks are a favored offense in pankration, the fighter must also be well prepared against attacks below the belt line. Low round kicks aimed at the outer thigh are often blocked with a toughened shin. Front kicks aimed at the lower body are intercepted in flight at the sensitive shin with a partially extended side kick (leg obstruction).

Parries (Deflections)

Parries are subtle, economical movements performed with a sharp slap of the palm to the inside or outside of or onto an oncoming blow or kick, with the intention of diverting the assault from its original path. Unlike the passive, rigid blocking techniques of some classical karate styles, the parry uses far less energy and allows redirection of force rather than absorbing a bruising bone-on-bone clash.

The key elements in the parry are timing and economy of motion. It is essential to parry at the last moment (late rather

Shin block.

Readiness positions.

A palm slap to the outside of a straight punch.

than early), when the blow is close to the body. Reaching out to parry an attack not only causes openings for counterhits, but also enables the opponent to alter the direction of his blow.

Either hand can be used to parry but never both at once. While one hand is deflecting the blow, the other hand (usually the front) is preparing to counter. As the parry is executed, it is often wise to swing the head and body slightly in the direction away from the strike. This provides an extra assurance that the attack will pass by harmlessly. A skillful striker with an excellent sense of timing has the ability to parry and punch simultaneously.

Parrying is an excellent means of defending against a wide variety of blows but is most effective for straight-line hits. Head shots can be parried to either the left or right, while blows aimed to the body are deflected downward. Front and side kicks can also be parried effectively by stepping back slightly or using lateral movement (sidestepping) to dissipate much of the kick's force. If executed perfectly, the parry can

Jamming a front kick with a side kick to the knee.

BASIC ANO COMBAT SKILLS

act to put the opponent off balance, placing him out of position to follow up with another attack.

Evasions

Another effective defense is the evasion, which allows freedom to both hands to counter while remaining in the attacking range. Evasion is much like parrying, where timing is so crucial. The movement is performed late rather than early, when the blow is almost upon you. In modern pankration, there are two basic evasions: slipping and ducking.

Slipping is a movement of the head to the inside or outside a straight-line blow, usually a hand attack. Slipping is very bewildering to an opponent and keeps him uncertain about landing his own shots. It also causes him to use up his strength: nothing in a fight is more tiring than missing blows because of the extra effort expended in recovering balance. On

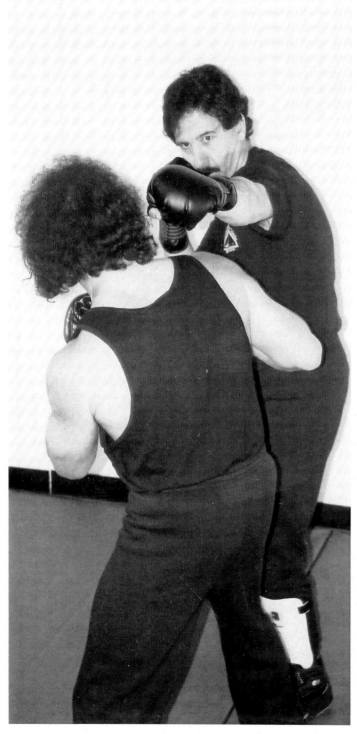

Inside slip.

Outside slip.

the other hand, by the use of the slip, a fighter can avoid a punch with the least amount of exertion and thus conserve strength and energy.

The most commonly used slips are those head movements to one side, just enough to let the punch pass by harmlessly. A fighter does not change the position of his feet, but bends his upper body to the right or left, far enough to carry the head out of line and allow the blow to go over his shoulder. He now finds himself in excellent position to unleash a blistering counterattack.

It is important to note that slipping is for leads to the head only. Body blows are taken on the arms, parried, or dodged. Also, a slip should never be initiated until the attack is on the way: it may be a trick to fake you out of position.

Ducking is an evasive move for swings or hooks to the head by lowering the head so that the blow passes over it. It is an effec-

Outside slip against a jab lead.

Ducking against a hook to the head.

Inside slip against a jab lead.

Ducking into a takedown.

43

tive means of avoiding a blow at the inside hand range because an opponent is made to miss without your losing your balance, thus leaving you in an advantageous position to counter.

The ability to duck improves your fighting prowess. The fighter who can duck effectively is hard to hit squarely and is generally able to fight closer to his opponent, always remaining within range for a countering strike or, in most cases, a takedown.

The only blows that ducking should be used against are swings and hooking blows directed at the head. Ducking does not involve bending at the knees. The fighter drops his body by bending forward at the waist. The guard is always brought in front of his face. Failure to do so leaves one vulnerable to uppercuts or knees to the face. A common ploy of the pankratiast is to avoid a head shot by ducking under it and to shoot for the legs to take the opponent down.

STRIKING TOOL DEVELOPMENT USING EQUIPMENT

Equipment is an integral part of pankration training. Just as a piece of training apparatus improves the output of any athlete, the use of functional devices serves to sharpen the striking tools of the full-contact fighter. It is particularly useful when a partner is unavailable to work out with, and it is an invaluable means for developing areas of weakness. Using a variety of devices, there is a systematic manner in which such specialized fighting skills as timing, power, speed, accuracy, distancing, and balance can be enhanced.

In pankration, equipment is treated as a real opponent rather than just a target to pound on. Some of these devices offer movement, by which precision in the blows is affected, as well as the timing to hit at the proper moment. Regardless of the type of apparatus used, it is imperative for the trainee not to forget about his guard when attacking, keeping himself well covered at all times. It is also important that the person or training partner holding the equipment is adept in its manipulation. He should act as a coach and sometimes as an opposing fighter, forcing you to get the best possible workout and to be aware of areas that need improvement. He should make you move, cover up, and hit from all possible angles.

The primary equipment employed in modern pankration training includes the heavy bag, speed bag, top-and-bottom bag, focus gloves, impact shield, offense-defense (O-D) mitts, and kick pads.

HEAVY BAG

The heavy bag, or *korykos*, is one of the most important pieces of training equipment used in modern pankration tool

The heavy bag.

Punching the heavy bag.

Kicking the heavy bag.

Heavy bag knee kick.

development. Pankratiasts have long used the heavy bag to develop kicking and punching force. Although today's standard models weigh about 80 pounds, the heavy bags employed in modern pankration training weigh approximately twice that. There are even larger bags that are filled with foam or water and tip the scales at more than 200 pounds. Some bags used in training, referred to as "banana bags," are 6 feet in length.

The main purpose of using the heavy bag is to develop power. Any striking tool can be applied with full force to the bag, which is normally stabilized by a partner or tied to the floor. When training with the bag, it is absolutely critical to consider the bag as an opponent rather than just a "dead" object to hit. Even though the bag is incapable of hitting back, the pankratiast must keep his guard up and stay well covered when attacking. By all means, he should use his imagination and treat the bag as if it is part of a real fight. Good movement, feinting, and variation in offense are emphasized in heavy-bag workouts.

Pankration heavy-bag training consists of 3 minutes of intense work followed by 1-minute breaks. It is important for the student of this art to develop the capability of delivering fluid hand and foot combinations, although it is good practice to isolate certain techniques, such as punching combinations, just kicks, or elbow and knee techniques, in some of the rounds.

SPEED BAG

The speed bag is an inflated leather bag attached by a swivel connection to an overhead rebound platform. The basic purpose of this apparatus is to develop speed of hand. In addition, it sharpens hand-eye coordination, timing, and rhythm, and strengthens the shoulder muscles.

The platform speed bag.

In a modern pankration palaistra, it is common to find speed bags of varying size. The physical stature, as well as the ability, of the trainee determines to some degree the appropriate size of the bag. Larger bags require more powerful blows to make them move, while smaller bags tend to move faster, thereby improving speed and coordination.

The influence of Western boxing on punching skills has resulted in pankratiasts' being trained to use the speed bag in the same way that a conventional boxer does. Beginning students stick to practicing their punches individually, and the more advanced practitioners employ many different striking patterns with a high level of proficiency.

Drill time with the speed bag is normally two or three rounds with a minute break in between each round. The duration per round is 3 minutes.

Speed bag striking.

DOUBLE-END BAG

The double-end bag (DEB) has been used in modern pankration training since its earliest beginnings. Filled with air, the leather-covered bag is circular in shape and is suspended at shoulder or face level (or higher) by a pair of springy elastic cords attached to the ceiling and floor. It comes in various sizes—8, 6, or even 4 inches in diameter—with the smaller, faster bag better suited for the more advanced practitioner.

The DEB is very difficult to hit consistently with any degree of accuracy at first. Unless it is struck perfectly straight and square, it bounces back at an unpredictable angle. The harder it is hit, the quicker and more forcefully it returns.

Next to a live sparring mate, the top-and-bottom bag is perhaps the best means of developing reflexes, timing, hand speed, and accuracy. Any type of strike is applicable: jabs,

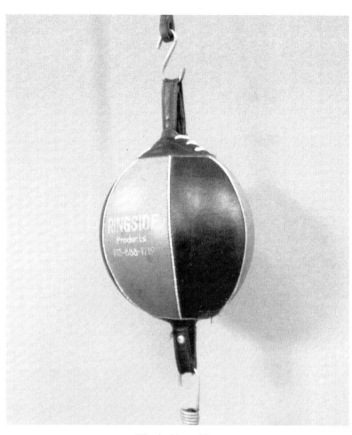

The double-end bag.

crosses, hooks, even uppercuts and elbows. Combination punches—primarily double jabs, the one-two, and the one-two-three—can also be employed once the mu tauist gains some experience in landing the single blows effectively.

As in the case of the heavy bag, this apparatus is treated by a pankratiast as a real opponent. Good footwork is used to control the bag's elusive movement, and defensive moves are applied as well as attacks. The DEB is struck forcefully and is evaded with a head slip as it caroms back. The pankratiast must be careful to maintain cover and work the bag with a broken rhythm. In other words, he should not punch the bag with a set pattern of blows and timing. The attacks should vary with a continuous alteration in the tempo of his actions.

Another version of this equipment used in training is the double DEB, which offers two targets to strike as well as a different rhythm for the fighter to adapt to. This is ideal for developing high-low and low-high punching combinations.

Drill time is typically three rounds with a minute rest between rounds. The duration of each round can be from 3 to 5 minutes, depending on ability.

Punching the double-end bag.

The double double-end bag.

48

FOCUS GLOVES (PUNCH MITTS)

One of the most versatile and extensively used training aids is the focus glove, which sharpens accuracy, timing, striking speed, and power in virtually any punch as well as some kicks.

The most effective use of the focus glove is in cultivating different punching (and kicking) combinations. In this drill, a holder wears gloves on both hands and continuously alters their positions, providing a constantly moving target. To get the most out of this type of training, you must work with a partner who is proficient in manipulating the gloves. He must keep you moving and persist in providing you with a variety of angles from which to strike. In modern pankration training, the holder functions as the "coach" and calls out combinations for the hitter to deliver, often using number sequences, such as one-two, one-two-three, etc.

Focus gloves come in various sizes. The smaller mitts are used primarily for punching drills, while larger sizes are for practicing elbow strikes. Drill time for focus glove training is variable. On the average, three rounds of 3 minutes each with 1-minute breaks are adequate.

Holding the gloves (a).

Lead jab to glove.

Rear cross to the glove.

Holding the gloves (b).

Elbow strike to the glove.

IMPACT SHIELD

The impact shield is an apparatus filled with a dense foam core that can contour itself to the human body. Its design enables the trainee to strike it full force without the shield's losing its original shape.

Round kick to the impact shield.

The impact shield.

Front thrust kick to the shield.

The impact shield is used to sharpen the body attack. The pankration kicking tools employed are the front thrust kick, both the lead hook and back-leg round kick, and kneeing. Punching techniques used include the reverse thrust and hooks and uppercuts with either hand. The partner holding the equipment positions the shield firmly to his chest and moves about rapidly, in and out, as well as laterally, providing a moving target for blows. He also rushes in frequently without warning, forcing a spontaneous reaction on the striker's part.

Drill time with the impact shield is two to three rounds of 3 to 5 minutes each. The trainees rest 1 minute between rounds.

OFFENSE-DEFENSE MITTS

O-D mitts are used to sharpen the offensive hand tools while simultaneously teaching good defensive skills, such as covering, slipping, and ducking. The value in this equipment is in forcing the puncher to concentrate on remaining well guarded at all times. The "coach" leads and counters with jabs and other blows to ensure that his partner fluidly integrates defense with attack.

KICK PADS

Kick pads are used by the modern pankratiast to harden the shins and knees. Full-power, follow-through round kicks with either leg are heavily favored techniques, although knee attacks are also practiced. For hard kick-punch combinations, the kick pad can be worn on one arm with a focus glove on the other hand.

The pads are leather arm shields about 1 foot in length and

Simultaneous parry and hit.

Holding the kick pads for body kicks.

Holding the offense-defense mitts.

Holding the kick pads for low kicks.

STRIKING TOOL DEVELOPMENT USING EQUIPMENT

Low round kick on pads.

Knee kick to pads.

filled with a dense foam. A rigorous session with this rock-hard equipment leaves the kicker bruised and swollen. Fitted with top handles and forearm straps, the pads are worn by a partner who fends off solid round kicks to both the lower and upper body. He turns the pads into each kick to offer greater resistance, thereby increasing the impact. The holder of the pad may also reach out occasionally with one of the mitts to tap the kicker in the head if his guard is too low. Even on the attack, the fighter must be aware of his defense. It is the trainer's responsibility to see that this lesson is properly learned.

In practicing the knee kicks, the hitter grasps the holder at the sides of his head in a clinch. The holder crosses the pads at his stomach and absorbs the pounding of multiple knee strikes while at the same time resisting the kicker's downward pull. If this was actual combat, the grip would work not only to pull the head down where it can be assaulted with the knees, but also as a chokehold reducing the flow of blood to the brain and further weakening the opponent. This training is consistent with pankration's emphasis on freely applying grappling in conjunction with striking techniques whenever possible.

UPRIGHT
GRAPPLING
SKILLS

Also essential to the pankratiast in stand-up fighting is grappling, which includes gripping, clinching, and taking an adversary off his feet. As mentioned earlier, upright grappling is *orthia pale* in Greek. Grappling is perhaps the earliest systematized combat form. It was refined in ancient Greece, where wrestling was first introduced into the Olympic Games of 708 B.C. The Roman Empire embraced wrestling with the same passion as the Greeks had and developed one of the main wrestling styles still used today, the Greco-Roman. The Romans adapted the sport to their own traditions and refined it even further, barring some of its more brutal features.

Grappling supplies the advantage to the "total" martial artist. Proficient grapplers have proven time after time that they can tie up and immobilize even the best punchers and kickers. Any martial art that does not include grappling and ground-fighting skills in its repertoire is not adequately preparing its followers for actual combat. There is a major difference, however, between wrestling and submission grappling. Wrestling's ultimate objective is to pin an opponent's shoulders to the mat, whereas submission grappling seeks to force an opponent to quit or suffer dislocation or even death.

Although grappling techniques are most often applied from close range or a clinch, they can also be initiated from longer distances by feinting to bridge the gap or following up a strike or kick. Grappling can also be employed effectively from this distance by drawing the opponent into leading and then using a grappling tool as a countering move. The modern pankratiast is trained to apply his knowledge of grappling from any range presented in a combat situation.

He does not rely solely on strength when grappling, but

Standing double shoulder lock.

also on proper technique and sensitivity to an opponent's movements. In addition, he thrives on exploiting the rival fighter's weaknesses and mistakes. The modern pankratiast is well aware that once on the ground, his foe will inevitably make a wrong move, and once that happens he, the pankratiast, will instantly take advantage of it.

Grappling, though extremely effective, demands extraordinary stamina and a great sense of leverage. Physical conditioning is imperative to effective grappling. Every muscle of the human body is used to the fullest degree. It requires the utmost balance, quickness, cardiovascular endurance, mental toughness, and kinesthetic awareness to control a larger opponent or reverse a seemingly hopeless position to one of advantage. Essential in grappling is knowing where one's body is in relation to an adversary. By establishing a solid base, a skillful grappler can turn his foe's energy against him, thus conserving one's own energy.

TRANSITIONING

Transitioning from striking range to close-quarter grappling requires that the pankratiast move in on the opponent at top speed and without warning. Any hesitation in the maneuver will most likely cause the opponent to avoid the attack or counter as the pankratiast "shoots" in low. It is important in closing the gap that the grappler does not absorb a solid blow on the way in. Sometimes, a preliminary hand feint or low kick is used to distract the opponent's attention from his lower body, which is being targeted for the assault. Another effective maneuver is to first disrupt the opponent's balance with a powerful low round kick to the legs. If the opposing fighter can be spun around, the pankratiast takes immediate advantage of this vulnerable situation to flank him from behind. Attacking a foe from the rear is a most advantageous position to be in for maximum grappling effectiveness. An opposing fighter must be careful not to expose his back to a trained pankratiast.

The clinch (tie-up).

Once the pankratiast has closed the distance, he applies a "clinch," gripping the opponent about the waist, legs, neck, or some other part of the body in preparation for taking the fight to the ground. This is sometimes referred to as the *tie-up* position.

RASSEIN APALY

Rassein apaly means taking an opponent "down" and placing him in a vulnerable position on the ground, whereby a follow-up offensive, either a strike or another grappling action, is normally used. The basic *rassein* techniques used in pankration are the leg tackle, waist lock, sweep, and throw.

Leg Tackle
The leg tackle is a takedown maneuver in which either one or both legs are grasped. The double-leg takedown is more effective because the opposing fighter has both legs under him; attacking only one leg requires more effort to bring the opposing fighter's body down to the ground. The single-leg takedown, on the other hand, is normally executed against a kicking offensive, when one's balance is centered on only one leg.

The "shoot."

In executing either takedown, the pankratiast lowers the center of gravity in his stance, while maintaining good balance, and then shoots in, securing his head on either side of the opponent's hips. Gripping the opponent's legs at either the knees or the thighs, he drives his upper body into the opponent's midsection or upper-leg area. The simultaneous action of scooping the legs while exerting pressure against the midsection results in an effective takedown. This technique can also be applied from behind the opponent. From this position, the ankles are gripped and the shoulder exerts pressure against the upper leg area.

Waistlock (*Mesolabe*)

Another common takedown technique of the pankratiast is the waistlock, wherein the opponent is gripped about the belt line from either the front or behind and then maneuvered to the ground, where he can be finished off. The legs are often used in this technique to further break down the opposing fighter's balance. The pankratiast wraps one of his legs around the opponent's leg at the knee or calf area while tripping him down. The heel often kicks sharply into the calf. The hands are wrapped about the midsection with the fingers interlocked behind the back. A variation of this technique is the reverse waistlock. This involves wrapping the arms about the opponent from his back and interlocking the hands in front of him. This technique is often employed to counter a leg tackle.

Double-leg takedown.

Single-leg takedown.

Front waistlock.

55

Front waistlock with trip.

Reverse waistlock (a).

Rear waistlock.

Reverse waistlock (b).

Sweeps

Also effective in taking an adversary down is sweeping a leg or the legs from under him. Sweeps are effective after a fighter's leg has first been seized or grabbed in a kicking assault. A slowly executed kick or any kicking attack to the midsection or higher is vulnerable to being seized by a good grappling technician. Once the leg is caught, a sweep to the supporting leg at the knee joint follows, with the intent of toppling the fighter.

1

Seize the opponent's kick.

Sweep.

2

Sweep the supporting leg at the ankle.

Throws

Throws are also employed to take an opponent to the ground. One such throwing technique is the headlock and hip throw. After securing a clinch from infighting range, the pankratiast often downs an opponent by grabbing him around the head while flipping him over the hip. This enables the pankratiast to maintain control of the opponent's head when the fight hits the ground.

The shoulder throw is an upper-body takedown in which the pankratiast locks an arm with an underhook and flips his adversary over his shoulder. This is accomplished with a quick pivoting movement of the feet and a forward dip at the waist. The adversary's arm is controlled at all times throughout the maneuver so that an armlock can be applied when the opponent is grounded.

Another throw that serves to finish a foe is the suplex, a maneuver in which the grappler executes a waistlock, gripping his opponent around the belt line from either the front (belly to belly) or behind (belly to back). You then fall backward (hyptiasmos) while shooting the opposing combatant over his shoulder and into the ground. The objective is not only to throw the opponent but also to crunch his head and shoulders from the resulting ground impact. This technique is a dangerous one: it could cause a broken neck if improperly executed.

UPRIGHT GRAPPLING SKILLS

1

Apply the side headlock.

2

Roll the hip under.

3

Drop at the waist.

4

Completion of the throw.

58

Shoulder Throw

1

Underhook to the opponent's arm.

2

Pivot your body and lift your opponent's body.

3

Drop at the waist and throw the opponent to the ground.

Front Suplex (Belly to Belly)

1

Apply the front waistlock.

2

Lift the opponent and fall back.

3

Throw the opponent overhead.

1

Apply a rear waistlock.

2

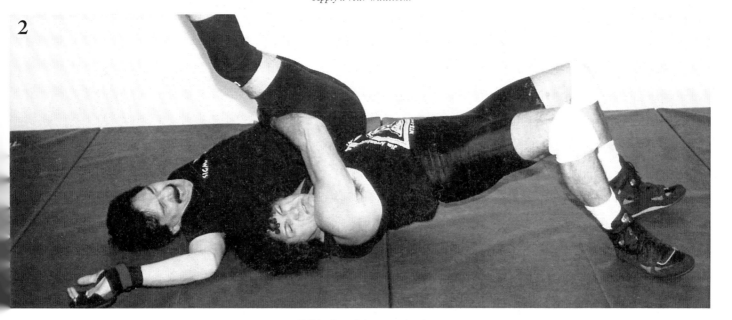

Fall back and throw overhead.

61

DEFENDING AGAINST TAKEDOWNS

The Sprawl

Other than attempting to catch the offensive grappler on the way in with an uppercut or knee strike, the basic defense of the pankratiast against leg takedowns or tackles is the sprawl. As the opponent initiates a shoot, this technique is exe-cuted by moving the hips out and away from the attacker's grasp by kicking one's legs straight back. The adversary's torso is then controlled by grasping his head or upper extremities. The opponent's body can then be shoved downward and underneath into a precarious position. The pankration practi-tioner may then spin onto his rival's back into the top-control position and unleash a more aggressive offensive.

Ssprawl used against a takedown attempt.

Sprawl Execution

1

Ready positions.

2

Opponent shoots for the legs.

3

Kick legs back and drop weight downward on the opponent.

4

Neutralize the opponent's movement on the ground.

SUBMISSION
AND
GROUND-FIGHTING
SKILLS

Sport pankration embraces the concept of submission, or forcing the opposing competitor to surrender. These techniques are applicable either when standing or on the ground. Kato pankration, the ground component of the combat system, usually finds either one or both combatants in a "down" position. It includes proper maneuvering, both offensive skills of striking and grappling, and sound defensive tactics. With a single-minded focus of attaining victory through any means possible, pankratiasts are trained to end a fight in a matter of seconds yet are prepared to do battle for long periods, if need be, to win. In many cases, they end the confrontation at ground level with either a relentless series of blows or a submission grappling technique.

Although a pankratiast is capable of ending a fight in an upright posture with a knockout blow or submission hold, there is at least an equal emphasis in sport pankration on going to the ground where grappling skills are combined with finishing strikes to defeat the opponent. This is especially the case when the fighters are standing toe-to-toe and too close for the striking tools to be effective. In this comprehensive art, the keys are to be ready for any type of opponent and to fit into any form of combative environment that might arise. While street fights frequently end up on the ground, mu tau, in the tradition of pankration, prepares its fighters for every possible situation.

In practice sparring or competition, once an opponent is taken down, the action continues on the ground, with each fighter attempting to force the other into signaling defeat verbally or by "tapping out" (i.e., slapping the mat twice). In an all-out fight, the ultimate intention of the pankratiast is to render the opponent either helpless or senseless.

Top-mounted elbow lock.

There are two basic offensive skills in kato pankration: submission grappling holds and finishing strikes. Of course, before successfully applying these skills, the pankratiast must be able to make the transition from the outside range to infighting and from a standing posture to the ground. Once on the ground, he must gain a position of control over his opponent.

GROUND CONTROL

Once the fight goes to the ground, the pankratiast attempts to obtain the best tactical position for subduing his opponent while smothering his ability to strike back effectively. A superb example of this is the top-control position, often referred to as the "mount" in other systems of self-defense that specialize in groundfighting. This maneuver often follows a takedown or knockdown from a strike, with the pankratiast working his way on top of the opponent and straddling his waist, locking his legs under his rival's upper thighs. In modern sport wrestling, this is similar to "riding" the back of an opponent.

The top-control position offers excellent placement for controlling the opponent's movements and launching an effective assault. If the opponent is facing upward, the mounter can pummel his opponent, raining downward punches and elbow strikes to the face. If he attempts to roll to the side to avoid the blows, the pankratiast responds by turning him onto his stomach and applying either a deadly chokehold or an armlock. Needless to say, this tactic of pinning an opponent is extremely difficult to escape from if it is properly executed and maintained.

Top-control position (front view).

Top control (back view).

The top position is an enviable place for the grappler. With the opponent facedown on the ground, the man on top uses his legs and his full weight so that his foe is pinned and cannot execute a "roll-out" maneuver or escape. From here the most obvious follow-up move is a rear stranglehold. If the opponent resists, an effective tactic is to yank his head back by pulling his hair and then applying the finishing grip about the throat.

For the fighter pinned on the bottom, this is one of the worst situations to be in. Due to the relative position of the shoulders and face, the fighter on top can easily strike the face of his opponent, but this is not possible for the man on the bottom. It is easier to strike downward than upward in this situation. In addition, the combatant in the top position has the advantage of leverage to gain more punching room and deliver more force behind his blows. The fighter pinned beneath cannot fully cock his arm because his motion is restricted by the ground.

Taking the opponent's back is the most effective form of tactical control in ground combat. Once a fighter has secured this position, his opponent is open to a number of submission attacks.

Side control.

Back mount.

Also effective for the top fighter is side control. Although this position does not allow an instant offense, it offers the advantage of controlling the opponent on the bottom and strategically moving into the top-mounted position, where a more efficient attack can be made.

A variation to the side-control position is to place a knee into the chest of the opponent. The use of the knee in this manner adds leverage for follow-up strikes or submission locks while neutralizing the opponent against the ground.

Knee in the chest.

SUBMISSION AND GROUND-FIGHTING SKILLS

FINISHING HOLDS

Joint Locks

Locks applied to an opponent's limbs have long been in pankration's grappling arsenal. Opportunities for applying joint locks are more frequent when one or both combatants are on the ground. Joint locks have only one purpose: to force the opponent to quit or else suffer a dislocated or broken limb. The joints most often attacked are the fingers, wrist, elbow, shoulder, knee, and ankle. The key is to twist or bend the limb against the joint to a point where the pain is unbearable for the opposing fighter. There are a number of variations of arm- and leglocks employed in pankration. The following is sampling of the major techniques.

Arm Bar

One of the most common limb locks is the arm bar. Although the technique is applicable from a standing position, it is most often employed when the combatants are on the ground. The arm bar can be used in a variety of ways and frequently follows the top-mounted position, with the fighter on the bottom facing up.

To apply the arm bar while the pankratiast is standing, the same basic principles are followed. The pankratiast grips the arm by the wrist while kneeling on the opposing fighter's head. He then leans his upper body backward, with the opponent's elbow braced against the crotch area.

Standing arm bar.

The arm bar can also be applied from a kneeling position, with the opponent on his back. The right hand stabilizes the shoulder while the left arm wraps under the elbow. Force is exerted by the pankratiast's pushing down on the shoulder while lifting up on the elbow joint.

Side arm bar (side view).

Side arm bar (top view).

Kneeling arm bar.

Executing the Side Arm Bar from Top Control

This is an excellent maneuver in which the mounted fighter swings to his left while gaining control of his opponent's arm. He then grips the arm by the wrist with both hands, holding it against his lower stomach area. In completing the move, the pankratiast then lies back, locking his legs over the neck and chest of the opponent to prevent him from rolling out. To exert pressure on the elbow joint, he elevates his pelvis while pulling the opponent's arm downward.

1

Top mount.

2

Swing left while maintaining a grip of the arm.

3

Fall back and squeeze the opponent's arm between your legs.

4

Hook your legs over the opponent's head and exert pressure on his elbow by raising your hips.

Hammerlock

The hammerlock is another effective finishing arm submission hold. In using this technique, the pankratiast employs both hands to fold the opponent's arm behind his back by gripping the elbow and wrist. Pressure is applied by yanking the trapped arm upward. The hammerlock can be applied with the pankratiast's back on the ground or from the top-control position.

Elbow Lock

The elbow lock is executed from either a kneeling or standing posture. It is an excellent street defense against an attempted rear choke. The positioning of the opponent's arm is critical: it must have the palm facing upward. Having grasped the wrist or lower forearm with both hands, place the opponent's elbow over the shoulder and then forcefully yank downward. The resulting action easily breaks the arm at the elbow joint.

Hammerlock from the back mount.

Hammerlock from the bottom position.

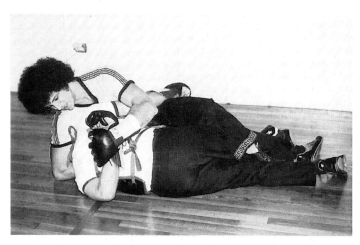

Hammerlock on the ground.

Standing elbow break.

Inverted Armlock

The inverted armlock is executed from the bottom position as the top-mounted fighter is attempting to gain the position of advantage. In this hold, the opponent's arm is pinned against the chest while your legs are wrapped about the shoulder of the trapped arm. The hips are raised to apply pressure.

Ankle Lock

In applying the ankle lock, the pankratiast simply grasps his opponent's lower leg at the ankle and twists it forcefully to either side. This technique is applicable when the fighter is upright or on the ground.

Standing ankle lock.

Inverted armlock.

Ankle lock on the ground.

Step-Over Toehold

A slight variation of the ankle lock is the step-over toehold. The pankratiast executes this submission technique by twisting the downed fighter's ankle as he quickly steps over his leg.

Double-Leg Lock

With the opponent on the ground and facing upward, the double-leg lock is an effective submission technique. It involves applying pressure by first lifting up on both of the opponent's legs. He is then rolled over and straddled by the pankratiast, who lifts up on his legs while leaning back. Not only does this cause extreme leg pain but can serve as a back-breaker as well.

Double-leg lock.

Leg Lever

From a sitting position on the ground, the leg lever is a painful submission lock whereby the pankratiast positions his own leg against the opponent's inner knee area, grips the lower leg at the ankle, and then applies pressure by forcing the trapped leg against his own knee.

Step-over toehold.

Leg lever.

SUBMISSION CHOKEHOLDS

Choking techniques have been favored tactics since pankration's earliest beginnings, with strangulation the most frequent cause of fatalities in matches. Arm chokes are the most popular, although the hands and even the legs can be applied. Once a firm grip has been secured about an opponent's throat, he will immediately submit before any further harm can be done to him.

Strangleholds can easily cause the victim to lose consciousness by preventing the flow of blood (i.e., with oxygen) to the brain. This is done by either compressing the carotid arteries on either side of the neck or putting pressure on the trachea (windpipe) in the front of the neck, from the Adam's apple to the top of the sternum.

Modern pankration training emphasizes the development of strong neck muscles to resist the damaging effects of a chokehold. Such a hold, however, is potentially lethal and difficult to escape from. Although it can be applied from a variety of positions, the chokehold is most commonly done from the top-control position.

Front Stranglehold

There are many chokes used by trained pankratiasts. One example is the front stranglehold, otherwise known as the "guillotine choke." This technique can be applied from either a standing or prone position.

Standing guillotine choke.

Guillotine choke on the ground.

Rear Choke

The most lethal pankration stranglehold is the rear choke, in which the opponent's back is to you and you throttle his neck with both forearms, one about the windpipe and the other exerting force against the back of the neck. This submission technique is primarily applied from the top-control position with the opposing fighter facedown.

Rear choke (front view).

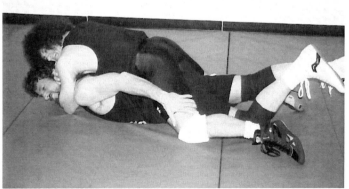

Rear choke (side view).

Klimakismos

The *klimakismos* (ladder trick) is a combination of rear choke and body scissors, which is often initiated from an upright position and eventually ends up with the fighters on the ground. In this technique, the pankratiast jumps on his adversary's back after either nudging him off balance with a leg kick or attaining the rear flank angle on him. This is an ancient finishing move and is well documented from the early days of the sport's inclusion in the Olympiads.

Ano klimakismos.

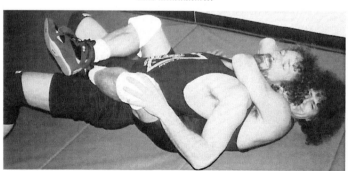

Kato klimakismos.

Side Choke

This submission stranglehold is applied from the side, with the pankratiast's body perpendicular to that of his opponent, who is on his back. The technique resembles a headlock, but has one major difference: the opponent's arm is pushed across the front of his neck. While one arm encircles the back of the opponent's neck, the top pankratiast tucks his head alongside the shoulder of the trapped arm, and with both hands interlocked brings pressure to the other side of the opponent's neck. Using body weight to push down on the trapped arm adds to the effectiveness of the choke.

Side choke.

Hand Chokes

Other choking tools available to the pankratiast include the front cross-arm choke and the single-hand choke. To be effective, the cross-arm choke should only be applied on an opponent who is wearing a shirt. In this way, the pankratiast uses the clothing to maintain a tight grip on his foe's throat. The hands are crossed, and pressure is exerted downward on both sides of the neck.

Single-hand choke.

Cross-arm choke.

Leg strangle from the bottom position.

Leg strangle against opponent on the ground.

The single-hand choke, on the other hand, is employed from a variety of positions, both standing and on the ground. It involves the use of one hand to clutch and squeeze the windpipe.

Leg Strangles

The legs are also used in applying submission chokes. Again, this technique is most frequently employed with either one or both combatants on the ground. It is a useful countering move against an opponent who is trying to get past the guard. As the fighter on top tries to pass the guard, the bottom man scissors his legs around his head, attempting to place the inside of the knee of one leg over the ankle of his other leg. One of the opponent's arms is also grasped with both hands to prevent an escape from the leg choke. Additional pressure is possible by releasing the arm, grabbing the back of the head, and pulling it forward while squeezing the thighs around the neck. The pressure exerted by the opponent's upper arm and the pankratiast's thigh diminishes the supply of blood to the opponent's brain, rendering him unconscious.

OTHER FINISHING TECHNIQUES

Ground Strikes

On the ground, pankration fighters are proficient in pummeling their opponent into submission from the top- or side-control positions. Whether the opponent is facing up or has his back turned, the pankratiast punches or elbows him in the head, face, or neck to subdue him. He also uses his knees to drop onto his adversary's body or head. If the pankratiast is on the bottom, he kicks the opponent in any open area. Ground strikes are effective in weakening the opponent in preparation for assuming a more advantageous position for subduing him and are used in conjunction with grappling holds.

Punching from the top mount.

Downward elbow strike to the neck.

When punching from the mount, a pankratiast often pins his opponent with his free hand. This prohibits the bottom man from elevating forward to grab the combatant on top and allows more room for the mounted fighter to deliver his strikes. The free hand can also be employed to trap or immobilize the opponent's arms so that he cannot block the blows.

Elbow strike to the face.

Punching from the back mount.

Once the pankratiast has secured the top-control position, he can also apply other submission grips about the head and neck areas other than a choke. A simple neck crank can be used, where the opponent's head is twisted violently to either left or right by grabbing his hair and chin.

Neck crank.

Another effective alternative is the chin lock, an immobilizing hold in which the pankratiast employs both hands to grip the chin of his adversary and force the head back while sitting on his opponent's back. Either of these techniques is potentially disabling.

Body punching from top control.

Knee drop to the head.

Chin lock.

77

BASIC GROUND-FIGHTING DEFENSES

In defending from the bottom position on the ground, the pankratiast often finds himself on his back. In such grappling-oriented styles as Japanese and Brazilian jujutsu, shootfighting, and pancrase, the term *guard* refers to a defensive ploy used against the top-mounted position. This form of ground defense can be applied from either close or long range. A variation known as the half-guard in ground-grappling circles is scissoring only one of the opponent's legs.

Before the opponent can firmly position himself in a fully mounted position, the bottom fighter attempts to keep the top man between his legs. He then scissors his legs about the opponent's waist, making it difficult for his opponent to gain the needed leverage to advance and effectively control him. A skilled groundfighter also pulls his opponent's head close to his chest, thereby nullifying his ability to launch an effective punch.

In defending from the bottom position, a pankratiast can assume control over his adversary and ultimately defeat him by executing an armlock or choke while in the supine posture. If the top man attempts to stand and launch downward punches to the face, the fighter on the bottom can use his feet to stop the blows by striking the adversary's biceps. This position also offers the option of playing a waiting game to conserve one's own energy while wearing down the opponent. The pankratiast then takes the offensive once exhaustion has forced a mistake from the opposing combatant.

HEEL KICKS FROM THE BOTTOM POSITION

In a long-range situation in which the pankratiast is on his back against a standing fighter attempting to move in, the feet become important tools. They can be employed to deliver front, side, and round kicks to the legs, body, or even the face of the aggressor. These techniques are used not only to hurt the opposition but also to secure a more advantageous strategic position from which to attack.

Ground scissors defense (closed guard).

Pulling back right leg.

Foot block from the bottom position.

Digging the heel into an opponent's back.

Side kick to the knee.

Heel to the groin.

Heel to the face.

The Elevator

The elevator is a basic defensive move used against a top-mounted fighter. The pankratiast, from the bottom position, simply performs a back bridge by elevating his hips using his head and legs. The objective of this technique is to jolt the opponent upward, thereby disrupting his balance and weight so that the bottom fighter can gain better position from which to defend himself.

The elevator.

Spartan Tactics

The militaristic Spartans attempted to simulate *panmachia*, or battlefield pankration, in their version of the sport. Today, these tactics are used solely for streetfighting. Included are ear and hair pulling for exerting control over an adversary and biting and eye gouging to gain release from an opponent's grip. To escape a rear choke, for example, pankratiasts often pin their chis against the top of their breastbones and use their hands to block a grip to the throat. They then reach for the adversaries' fingers and bend them back forcefully. In gouging an opponent's eyes, either thumbs or extended fingertips are used.

Spartan Tactics

Finger bending.

79

Spartan Tactics: Gouging and Biting on the Ground

Olympic pankration rules forbade gouging and biting. The Spartans, however, were particularly fond of these tactics and freely employed them in their local warlike contests, especially in fierce ground combat. Ripping an ear with the teeth was common, as was thumbing and jabbing the eyes.

Hair pulling.

Thumb strike.

Finger jab.

Ear pulling.

Biting.

CHAPTER 7

COMBAT STRATEGY

Fighting is often thought of as one combatant simply overpowering the other. In reality the winner in battle is not necessarily the stronger individual. Victory is often achieved by the fighter with better technique and strategy. It is a fact that a smaller man can overcome one who relies totally on physical attributes alone. He who can out-think his opponent always has the advantage. Of all the personal weaponry available to a combat athlete the most powerful is the mind.

Strategy is of paramount importance to the modern pankratiast. Applying one's offensive skills in a sound tactical manner is considered the highest level of proficiency in the art, one requiring superb technique as well as exceptional mental aptitude. These tactics include setups, combinations, and counterattacks.

SETUPS

A setup is a means of disrupting an opponent's timing while simultaneously inducing a defensive reaction, thereby creating an opening for an attack. Setups are based on the effective use of feinting.

Feinting is based on the element of surprise, using some form of body or limb movement to deceive an adversary. Feints use cunning and technical deception to provide a false impression of your intended action. Then, as your opponent makes his predicted response, your attack finds the opening in his defense. When feints are mixed with direct attacks and combinations, the opponent is constantly baffled as to what is real and what is not.

The feint is a partially committed blow or kick that appears to be the start of a sound offensive tactic but is real-

Top-mounted striking.

High hand feint induces a high block.

ly intended to elicit a defensive reaction from the opposing fighter. His reaction then creates an opening for another type of attack.

Feinting only sets up momentary openings. To score effectively on these exposed targets necessitates instant reflex action as well as a foreknowledge of what openings will be created by certain feints. Such familiarity demands practice—only through the actual use of many feints against many different types of fighters can a general reaction tendency be determined.

A feint cannot look like a feint; it must appear to be an actual attack. The only way to deliver a successful indirect offensive is to be able to feint convincingly and thus obtain the maximum reaction from your opponent. If your foe does not respond accordingly, your feinting is not being properly executed. When feinting be fully aware of your opponent and his reaction. He must react in such a way that he actually feels threatened by that preparatory move.

Probably the most difficult part in applying a feint is in the perfection of one's sense of timing. The execution must allow for a slight pause to enable the opponent to react prior to the delivery of the actual attack. It must be done such that he is unable to determine what technique is on its way. Repetitious drilling on this pause is crucial to apply the feint effectively.

The initial movement must permit you to gain critical distance between you and the opposition. This preparatory maneuver throws off your rival's timing as you follow up with the intended technique.

Low hand feint induces a low block.

Low kick feint induces a low block.

Some Basic Setups

Low Jab Feint to High Lead Hook

From the ready poses, induce your opponent to lower his hands by faking a jab to the body. Once an opening in the high line presents itself, deliver a solid lead hook to the jaw.

Jab Feint to Double-Leg Tackle

This is an example of a high-distraction setup of a low attack, in this case, a grappling takedown.

Ready positions.

Ready positions.

Lead with a low jab feint.

High jab feint.

Shift to a high hook.

Shoot for the legs.

COMBAT STRATEGY

4

Grip both legs behind the knees.

5

Drop the opponent on his back.

High Jab Feint to Low Back-Leg Kick

From a ready position, force the opponent to raise his guard with a feint jab to the face. Once he adjusts his defense, step in with a back-leg round kick to the thigh.

1

Ready positions.

2

High jab feint.

3

Round kick to the legs.

Contemporary pankratiasts are well schooled in delivering their offensive tools in combinations. A combination is best described as two or more attack techniques delivered in fluid succession. The attacks flow from one into another naturally, the objective being to overwhelm the opponent with a flurry of moves without giving him time to react effectively. For example, it is difficult to score with a single blow against a fighter with a good, airtight defense. By combining successive techniques into a natural sequence, a heavier burden is placed on a defense. Well-planned and executed combinations get through even the tightest guard.

In stand-up fighting one blow may not stop an opponent, but an accumulation of strikes often does the job. In pankration combinations can consist of a series of striking techniques, grappling maneuvers, or a blend of strikes and grappling. Most of the striking combinations employ the hands. These punching combinations are cleverly orchestrated sequences, with each opening creating another. In all cases, each blow or movement in the sequence is intended to land or uncover gaps in as defense for follow-up attacks. This method of taking the offensive requires economical motion, tight and alert defensive covering, speed and surprise, and confidence in execution. To develop effective combinations, the pankratiast begins by perfecting a series of basic moves that easily follow each other. The initial technique of a combination is normally the most important because it sets up the opponent. If the first blow dazes him or causes him to drop his guard, the follow-up strikes are certain to land cleanly and hurt him.

The first technique must always be executed explosively and with excellent timing to catch the opposing fighter in a moment of weakness. This might be as he is altering his guard, if he loses concentration for an instant, or if he has been distracted by a false movement. It is also essential to begin combinations with a lead jab, since it is closer to the targets and easier to land.

Whereas speed and untelegraphed motion are crucial factors in successfully landing combinations, the next blow should begin without delay as the preceding one is being retracted. Distancing is also of paramount importance when attempting combination strikes. Each technique in the series should be able to make contact with the adversary by either taking a slight step forward or back. Beginning a combination from too far out only allows your opponent greater time to counter or catch you with a shot while you are in the process of stringing your blows together.

Striking Combinations

There are literally hundreds of striking combinations in modern sport pankration. The following is but a sampling of some of the major ones. In most sequences the combination is initiated with the lead jab, which serves to set up the heavier blows of the series.

1

Ready positions.

2

Lead jab to the face.

3

Rear cross to the jaw.

Lead Uppercut/Rear Elbow Strike (Infighting)

1

Ready postions.

2

Uppercut to the solar plexus.

3

Rear elbow strike to the head.

Jab/Lead Hook

1

Ready positions.

2

Close the gap with a jab to the face.

3

Pivot hips for leverage.

4

Lead hook punch to the head.

Jab/Rear Thrust/Lead Hook

1

Ready positions.

2

Close the gap with a jab.

3

Deliver a rear thrust to the face.

4

*Finish the combination
with a lead hook to the head.*

1

Ready positions.

2

Lunging jab to the face.

3

Switch to low hook for ribs.

4

Pivot the body outward.

5

Hook to the head.

1

Ready positions.

2

Lunging jab to the face.

3

Rear thrust to the face.

4

Clinch the neck.

5

Drive knee into the solar plexus.

Strikes to Takedowns

Sometimes a transition to grappling range is set up by a striking technique. The following are some basic examples.

Low Front Kick to Waistlock

In this series the takedown follows a front thrust kick to the knee.

Ready positions.

Lead with a low front kick.

Blitz in with a waistlock.

Leg Kick to Rear Waistlock Takedown

From readiness, take the offensive with a low kick to the legs. With the opponent spun off balance from the impact of the kick, close with a rear waistlock. Wrap one leg around his legs and force him face-forward to the ground.

Ready positions.

Lead with a low round kick.

Apply a rear waistlock with a trip.

Take the opponent's back.

Takedowns to Follow-Up Submissions

Grappling combinations usually consist of a takedown or throw followed by a submission hold or finishing strikes. Once the fight goes to the ground, you must be skilled in continuing the relentless attack.

Front Waist Tackle to Top Mount to Finishing Strikes/Choke

Once you gain a waistlock clinch and take the fight to the ground, maneuver into the top-control position and unleash repeated punches to the face. If the opponent turns to avoid the strikes, flip him onto his stomach and apply a rear choke.

Shoot in under the high jab.

Apply a front waistlock.

3

Bring your left leg behind the opponent's leg.

4

Once on the ground, secure the top mount and strike to the opponent's face.

5

The opponent rolls to the side to avoid blows.

6

Turn the opponent over onto his stomach.

7

Apply a rear submission choke.

Shoulder Throw to Side Armlock on Ground

Using an arm throw to topple the opponent, continue to hold on to his arm, applying a submission arm bar from the side once you are on the ground.

1

Tie-up position.

3

Grip his arm and bend forward.

2

Underhook the opponent's right arm and position your hip under his waist.

4

Toss opponent over hip.

5

Complete the throw to the ground.

6

Maintain hold of the opponent's arm.

7

Drop to the left knee.

8

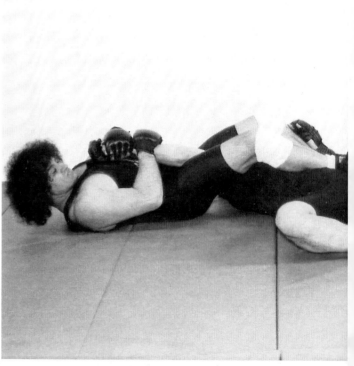

Fall back into a side arm bar.

Rear Leg Tackle to Leg Lock

Close the gap by shooting for the legs and quickly spin to the rear flank position. Grip the opponent's legs at the lower shins and drive him face-forward into the ground by pushing against the back of his knees with your shoulders. Once he is down, maneuver on top of his legs and apply a leg lever to force him to submit.

1

Ready positions.

2

Shoot for the legs.

3

Flank to the back of the opponent.

4

Grip his legs at the shins.

93

5

Pull back on his legs while pushing your shoulder into his upper thigh.

6

Maintain a grasp of the opponent's right leg
and slip your left leg behind his knee joint.

7

Lean in, putting pressure on his knee.

Spear to Throw to Submission Choke

In this series, a strike is used to close the gap for a take-down and follow-up finishing hold. After delivering an eye jab, move in with a hip/headlock throw. Once on the ground, roll the opponent's shoulder in front of his face and interlock the fingers under the side of his neck. Apply a side choke by leveraging your weight in pushing the head against the shoulder and squeezing with the arms against the other side of his neck.

1

Ready positions.

2

Lead with a strike to the eye.

3

Move in and apply a side headlock.

4

Execute a hip throw.

5

Drop down, maintaining side control.

6

Apply a side choke.

COUNTERATTACKS

A counterattack is a retaliatory blow or grappling action given in reply to an opponent's lead. It is not purely a defensive tactic but is a means of taking the offensive once the opponent's attack has first been thwarted. Counters are broken into two areas: counterstrikes and countergrappling. In grappling, when a takedown or submission maneuver is countered, it is often referred to as a *reversal*.

Counterstrikes

There are three elements essential to effective counterstriking: the opponent's lead, the method of avoiding the lead, and the retaliation itself. Against punches, for example, a blow with the forward hand exposes the front part of the body, while a rear-side blow exposes all of the upper trunk.

In avoiding leads a fighter must decide instantaneously whether to parry, block, apply an evasive move, or attempt to beat the opponent to the attack. Parrying leaves only one hand to counter but has the advantage in mu tau pankration of being used concurrently as a trap to inhibit the opponent's continued use of that arm. Such evasions as slipping and ducking allow two-fisted counters.

An effective counter sometimes depends on drawing, or luring the opposing fighter into leading. By offering him what appears to be an opening, you force the opponent into "taking the bait." Even though it is a deliberate error, it must never appear this way to him, since an experienced fighter seldom, if ever, falls prey to a "setup."

Drawing the attack is a premeditated action, and its success depends on enticing your rival into attacking at the openings being presented. Examples of drawing include lowering the rear-hand guard to expose the head, lowering the lead hand for head exposure, and holding the guard extremely high to invite a body attack. The following are some basic counterstriking tactics.

Front Shin Block to Back-Leg Round Kick to Thigh

In this counter the fighter on the left attacks with a leg kick, which is blocked with the shin. The defender quickly retaliates with a back-leg round kick to the thigh.

1

Ready positions.

2

Block a round kick with the shin.

3

Counter with a round kick to the thigh.

Slip Jab to Side Kick to Knee

1

Ready positions.

2

Slip inside jab.

3

Counter with a downward side kick.

1

Block hook to head.

2

Counter with a lead elbow to the head.

3

Finish with a rear elbow strike.

Reversals (Countergrappling)

A reversal is a grappling maneuver used to alter the control situation in a fight. It is actually a counter to a takedown attempt, strategic position, or hold.

Reversals require an excellent sense of leverage. Once the fighter feels a shift in balance so that the opponent's weight is distributed in one direction, he "rolls" in that direction to gain a better position. This same principle also applies to applying holds. The key is to go *with* the direction of the exerted force, not against it.

Most reversals in sport pankration are employed against either a top-mounted fighter or one who has attempted a throw or takedown maneuver. The following are some basic examples of countering with grappling and reversing the control factor.

Forward Roll to Mount to Choke

From the ready position, the pankratiast on the left dodges and parries a lunging straight lead and applies a rear waistlock. The lock is reversed by grabbing the opponent's hands, tucking your chin down, and rolling forward. Complete the maneuver by obtaining top control and finish the opponent by choking him out, using the opponent's own shoulder to exert pressure against his throat.

1

Ready positions.

2

Opponent sidesteps a lunging jab.

3

Opponent applies a rear waistlock.

4

Trap his arms and dip forward.

5

Drop to your knees and throw your opponent forward.

6

Apply a choke from top control.

Trapped-Arm Roll (Choke Escape) to Armlock

While on your knees against a mounted opponent who is attempting a rear choke, pin your chin against your breastbone. Then trap the opponent's arm while doing a side roll. Maintain your grip on his arm and apply pressure against the elbow joint.

1

Opponent has the back mount and attempts a rear choke.

2

Trap his right arm.

3

Roll to the right.

4

Throw the opponent off your back.

5

Maintain control of his arm and lock at the elbow.

99

Arm-Throw Counter to Klimakismos

From a clinch, the opponent attempts a shoulder throw. Maneuver onto his back while using your free hand to push against his lower back. This will interrupt his momentum in throwing you. Then take him to the ground with a rear stranglehold while applying a leg scissors about his waist.

1

From the tie-up position.

2

Opponent attempts a shoulder throw.

3

Place left hand on his lower back.

4

Drop to one knee and take down the opponent.

5

Fall back into klimakismos.

Sprawl to Top Control to Choke

Against a leg takedown attempt, execute a sprawl by kicking the legs back and dropping your weight on top of the opponent. Quickly spin to the right and obtain the top-control position. Snake the left arm underneath the opponent's throat and end the conflict with a rear choke.

1

Opponent shoots for the legs.

2

Kick legs back and grip the opponent's upper torso.

3

Spin to the right.

4

Move into a back mount.

5

Force the opponent to submit with a rear choke.

Counter Headlock/Hip Throw with Belly-to-Back Suplex

Against the opponent who charges in and grabs you about the head in preparation for a hip throw, maneuver behind him and clinch him around his waist. Throw him backward with a suplex. In this countering move your stomach should be making contact with his back.

1

Ready positions.

2

Opponent moves in to wrap his arm around your neck.

3

Slip your head under his arm.

4

Flank the opponent and grip him around his waist.

5

Execute a belly-to-back suplex by falling back and crashing the opponent to the ground.

Counter Waistlock with Front Suplex to Top Control to Strikes

Against an opponent who shoots for a front waistlock, grab him about the neck in a guillotine choke and then quickly roll back, throwing him to the ground. As he lands on his back, roll on top of him, pin him by using the left hand on his throat to nullify his movement, and unleash strikes.

1

Opponent shoots in low.

2

Grip the upper body with both arms.

3

Fall back and throw the opponent.

4

Elevate your hips.

5

Roll up over the top of the opponent.

Counter Shoot with Choke from Top Mount

Against a shoot for the legs, sprawl the opponent and spin to your left into a top mount. Deliver punches to the body and head to weaken him. Finish with a rear choke.

1

Ready positions.

Secure a mounted position.

2

Kick back legs and use arms to control the opponent.

7

Grip the throat with the left hand and punch with the right fist.

3

Drop weight on top of the opponent.

4

Spin to the left and deliver body punches with the left fist.

5

Secure full mount and punch to the face.

6

Finish with a rear choke.

Counter Kick with Sweep to Leg Lock to Strikes

Against a kick, seize the leg and sweep the supporting foot at the calf. Maintain the grip on the foot and pull back on it. The knee is wedged behind the back of the opponent's knee. Deliver finishing elbow strikes to the head.

1

Opponent leads with a front kick to the body, which is seized.

2

Sweep the supporting leg while maintaining a grip of the other leg.

COMBAT STRATEGY

3

Roll the opponent onto his stomach and apply an ankle lock.

4

Continue the ankle grip with the left hand and cock the right arm.

5

Deliver downward elbows to the head.

Counter Takedown with Knee
Strike and Standing Guillotine Choke

Against a takedown attack, pull back the right leg while maintaining control of the opponent's movement by gripping the back of his head. Deliver a knee to the face and then slip the left arm under his chin and apply a guillotine chokehold. Lean back to exert maximum pressure on the throat.

1

Opponent shoots in for a leg tackle.

2

Grab the opponent's head and withdraw the right leg.

3

Deliver a knee strike to the face.

4

Finish with a guillotine choke.

Defending from the Bottom Position

Against a top-mounted fighter who is punching at your head, position your right heel against the inside of his upper thigh and the left knee into his chest to halt his advancement. Use both hands to trap his left arm. Push your heel into the biceps of his punching arm. Quickly roll to your right while slipping the left leg over his shoulder. Holding the arm at the wrist, squeeze both legs and push upward against the elbow joint to make the opponent tap.

1

Top-mounted opponent prepares to punch.

2

Grip the right arm with both hands and push your foot into the biceps of the opponent's left arm.

3

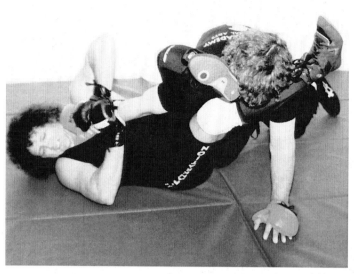

Slip your left leg over the opponent's shoulder while maintaining a grip on the right arm and roll to the right.

4

Squeeze the opponent's arm between both your legs and exert pressure on the elbow joint.

Counter Standing Ankle Lock with Takedown and Toehold

The opponent attempts a standing ankle lock against his grounded rival. Before he can fully apply the hold, spin to your left in the direction of the force being exerted and wrap your legs around both his legs. Grip his right ankle with both hands and sweep him off balance. As he falls to the ground, slip your right leg over his body to neutralize his ability to escape. Lean back and execute a toe lock to force him to tap out.

1

Opponent attempts a standing ankle lock.

2

Roll to the left and wrap your legs around his legs.

3

Grab the ankle closer to you while sweeping him down.

4

Continue the ankle grip and slip your right leg over his body.

5

Lean back and pull back his toes.

Countering Standing Headlock

Against a side head lock, punch the opponent's thigh to gain release. Slip behind him and take his back. Apply a rear choke. If he defends by tucking his chin against his chest, pull back on his head using his hair to expose the throat. Then fall back, hooking your legs around his waist.

1

Against a side headlock, cock the right fist.

2

Punch the opponent in his thigh.

3

Slip behind and take his back.

4

While you are clamping on a rear choke, the opponent defends.

5

Pull his head back using his hair.

6

Fall back and hook your legs about his upper legs.

Passing the Guard

If your opponent has you trapped in his open guard, lean forward and punch to the head. Quickly turn to the right while trapping his right leg in your arms. Then step over his body and sit back to exert pressure in the knee lock.

1

The opponent has you in his open guard.

2

Lean forward and cock the right fist.

3

Punch at the face.

4

Pivot to the right and grip his left leg while you are stepping over his body.

5

Start putting pressure on his knee by bending back.

6

Sit back into the knee lock.

111

Reversing the Side Headlock on the Ground

The opponent has secured a side headlock while you two are ground fighting. Press your left forearm against the side of his neck and roll your left leg over his hip. Mount his back and yank his head backward to open the throat. Bring him to submission with a rear choke.

3

1

The opponent has a side headlock while on the ground.

Mount back and slip your arm under the opponent's chin.

4

2

Press your forearm on his neck and roll your leg over his hip.

Apply a rear choke.

SPARTAN DISCIPLINE

An important aspect in the study of pankration is a traditional Greek code of conduct referred to as *Spartan discipline*. This discipline, inspired by the ancient inhabitants of Sparta, was observed by all warriors and athletes. It was necessary in preparing the mind and body to successfully cope with the demands of life-or-death combat in the arena or on the battlefield. Today, Greek martial art imparts Spartan discipline to its followers, applying it to both no-holds-barred combat in the street and the continual striving for perfection of one's craft. According to the ancient Greeks, the mental and physical aspects of an athlete are inseparable; one cannot exist or function without the other. To prepare for combat requires that the pankratiast aspire to be a highly conditioned athlete and to experience realistic simulations of combat in his training.

CONDITIONING EXERCISES

Sheer physical fitness is a significant part of the martial arts, but a rigorous conditioning program is often neglected, with the practitioner seeking to perfect the combat techniques themselves. To a pankratiast, perfecting the tools is certainly essential but so is maintaining or upgrading his physical condition. If there is truly any "secret" to acquiring martial arts proficiency, then it is hard training. Proper training is a means of disciplining the mind and building the body. It involves sufficient rest, good nutrition, and plenty of exercise. A pankratiast will discover that his kicks, strikes, grappling skills, and staying power will attain peak efficiency if he is fit.

A martial artist must be aware of those exercises that benefit his skills and others that might hinder his progress. Lifting

Jumping rope.

extremely heavy weights, for instance, is not advised because this might be detrimental to both speed and flexibility, vital attributes of a trained pankratiast. The exercises emphasized in pankration can roughly be divided into three groups: those that loosen and limber the body, those that supply endurance to the muscular and cardiovascular systems of the body, and those that enhance muscular strength.

Warm-Ups

Athletes always warm up before a game or contest. They are well aware that to perform well, they must prepare their bodies to undergo rigorous physical activity. Any form of strenuous exercise that taxes muscles, tendons, ligaments, heart, and lungs should be preceded by well-planned warm-up exercises and followed by similar cooldown exercises.

Because it is a vigorous form of exercise, any full-contact combative art places stress on the human body. To withstand such stress, muscles must be made loose and supple, and blood must start pumping at an exercise level. Large amounts of oxygen must be taken into the body and carried by the bloodstream throughout the system.

In like fashion an athlete must be careful to taper off his exercise, not come to an abrupt halt. Runners usually jog a slow lap; swimmers take a last swim. This is the cooldown phase, a critical link between rigorous activity and relative calm.

An average warm-up period might last approximately 10 to 15 minutes, but this varies according to the climate. Mu tau training features a small group of simple warm-up exercises that are effective in stepping up circulation, limbering certain muscles, improving mobility, and readying the body for the rugged demands of the training regimen to follow. A pankration trainee avoids rushing through this warm-up phase, unlike many athletes. He will work through them thoroughly to gain the most beneficial results.

The warm-ups performed in modern pankration training include neck rolls designed to loosen the neck muscles. The head is rotated fully in both directions, gently at the start with a gradual increase in range of motion and forcefulness. Trunk twisting stretches the lateral muscles of the midsection (obliques) and loosens the muscles of the chest and shoulders. An empty bar is held across the shoulders in this exercise to enhance the ballistic whipping action at the waist.

A good warm-up for limbering the lower back and hips is the cat stretch, basically a push-up movement where you slide the body along the floor as far as possible before arching your back at the completion.

Another good warm-up is the trunk bend. By bending the upper body as far back as possible, the lower back muscles are loosened. Bending forward from the waist and grasping the ankles while touching the head to the knees stretches the rear thigh muscles.

Leg-stretching exercises are also part of warming up. All athletic endeavors requiring heavy use of the legs incorporate stretching exercises into their conditioning programs to prevent pulled muscles and tendons and for greater flexibility.

Neck rolls.

Trunk twisting.

Cat stretch.

Front trunk bends.

Rear trunk bends.

Research has proven that regular stretching can bring about improvements in flexibility, accuracy, speed of movement, agility, and balance. Just as important, stretching increases tissue elasticity, thereby decreasing the likelihood of injury. Strained muscles impede movement, but more important they lead to torn muscle fibers. Once torn, inflexible scar tissue often fills the afflicted area, leaving it weak and always susceptible to further damage.

Although there are a variety of stretches, the slow-hold form, or static stretch, is best. It is done by slowly stretching until a slight feeling of discomfort appears and then holding that position for a period of 15 to 30 seconds.

Flexibility training can be performed with or without a partner. Some of the solo stretches include frontal bends on a bar and splits with a power stretch apparatus. When working with a partner, elevating the leg as high as possible to the side is an effective method of improving flexibility, as is having him apply pressure as you bend forward to touch your chin to the floor.

Front stretch on bar.

High side stretch with partner.

Power stretcher.

Splits with partner.

Endurance Training

The best endurance exercise is running. A normal running schedule for a serious mu tau pankration student is four to five days weekly, covering a minimum distance of 3 miles in 24 minutes or less. This includes different tempo and strides, usually mixing in full-speed bursts (sprints) for several yards with easier jogging. By running religiously, the pankratiast conditions virtually all the muscles in the body, as well as the heart, lungs, and circulatory system.

Another endurance exercise emphasized in the modern pankratiast's training agenda is jumping rope, or rope-skipping. Jumping rope not only develops stamina and strong leg muscles but also brings about improvement in footwork, making the pankratiast "light" on his feet.

Jump rope exercise is controlled by the clock. In the early stages, it is done for two, or perhaps three, 3-minute rounds with 1-minute breaks. After greater skill and dexterity are achieved, the rest periods can be omitted, and the pankratiast can jump rope for 10 to 15 minutes nonstop.

There are basically two rhythms employed when jumping rope. These rhythms relate primarily to the speed with which the rope is swung. Both rhythms can be performed either in series or in combination. The most frequently used rhythm is single-time, or pepper rhythm. With this rhythm, the trainee makes a slight jump with each pass of the rope. Double-time rhythm requires a very fast swinging rope, as well as a much higher jump. The rope makes two complete turns to pass twice beneath the feet with each jump.

Once the rope-jumping rhythms are perfected, the trainee must become well versed in various patterns. From these, thousands of unique and creative routines can be devised by each student.

Strength Training

The Greeks have long believed in using resistance to develop strength. Certain vase paintings show Athenian athletes exercising with very light weights for the purposes of improving their muscle tone and quickness. The tradition continues today.

All movement is a result of the contraction of a muscle or a group of muscles to produce movement. The intensity of a strike, kick, or grappling maneuver is determined by the joint effort of various muscle groups coordinating the technique. For example, a swift, powerful punch is not the product of just the arms. In many cases the power behind a punch is generated in the legs, by a stance or a shifting of weight. It is then transmitted through the torso by a slight waist twist and is amplified by the arms, back, and shoulders. Essentially, a dev-

Running is a great conditioning exercise.

Jumping rope is another great endurance exercise for the modern pankratiast.

astating punch or kick is the result of synchronized body movement rather than kinetic strength itself; however, since a certain degree of strength greatly enhances the end result, a pankratiast should strive diligently to develop overall muscular strength.

The type of exercise appropriate for readying one's muscles for combat is quite different from that used to build muscle size. In any area of the fighting arts, the object is to harden and tone the muscles rather than building size or mass. The key to combat success lies in the application of efficient muscle power.

Strength training in mu tau consists of using either free weights or body weight to supply the resistive force necessary to increase bodily strength. Contrary to the old way of thinking in the martial arts, weight training is advantageous in developing power without loss of speed. Be cautious, however, not to build large, bulky muscles, which might sacrifice swiftness and flexibility. The key element in proper weight training for combat purposes is not in how much weight you can lift but in doing the exercises correctly in full, smooth repetitions. For this reason, today's pankration trainees lift relatively lighter weights in high repetitions (three sets of 12 to 15 "reps" is a minimal workout for an exercise that isolates a specific muscle group).

The following exercises are representative of pankration strength training. The first set is designed to develop the neck and stomach muscles for the purpose of taking head and body shots in combat. The second group concentrates on improving punching power and upper-body strength by developing those muscles directly used in both striking and grappling techniques.

Neck lifts with harness.

Neck and Abdominal Exercises

In a full-contact combative art, powerful neck and abdominal muscles are necessary to withstand the shock impact of solid blows to the head and midsection. Boxers who suffer from frequent knockdowns or knockouts, referred to as having a "glass jaw," can attribute their inability to take a punch on the chin to weak neck muscles. If the abdominal region of a fighter is not conditioned, he can easily get the wind knocked out of him from either a single well-placed blow or the cumulative impact of multiple blows.

One means of building a strong neck is to perform isotonic neck lifts using a head strap and weighted plate. An alternative method is to take a position on your hands and knees and attempt to lift your head upward against some immovable object, such as a heavy bag or a partner who uses both hands to supply resistance.

Neck bridging exercises are also part of the pankratiast's training regimen, as they are in all combat systems oriented to grappling. In the front bridge, the trainee places the top of his head on the mat and arches his back so that the feet and head are the sole supporting points. In the back bridge, the exercise is similar except that the trainee takes a supine position on the mat. The neck muscles are developed in both positions by rolling the head back and forth.

Neck lifts with partner resistance.

Front bridge.

Crunches.

Back bridge.

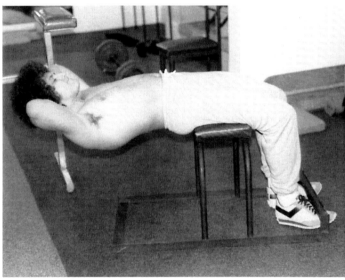

Sit-ups using a Roman chair.

There are several exercises to strengthen the abdominals, the most popular being crunches. Crunches are best for hardening the upper stomach muscles (*rectus abdominis*). In pankration training, this movement is always performed slowly with the upper body descending more slowly than it ascends. More benefit is gained by doing them in a slow and deliberate manner because continuous tension is concentrated on the abs. The *quality* of the movement is more important in this exercise than the *quantity*. In other words, it is not the number of repetitions, as many tend to think, but rather the way in which the crunching movement is done.

To perform a crunch, you can use a special device designed to reduce the strain on the neck and concentrate all of the effort on the stomach. With the hands placed on both sides of the unit, raise the upper body forward to a half-sit-up position. Repeat this movement several times until you feel a burning sensation in the abdominal area.

Other excellent abdominal building exercises are sit-ups and leg raises. Sit-ups, like crunches, work the upper abdominals, whereas leg raises develop the lower muscles of the stomach, perhaps the most underworked area in the human body. Sit-ups are more productive when using a slant board.

In performing leg raises, the equipment required includes a flat bench and ankle weights. The degree of difficulty in performing leg raises is regulated by how straight the legs are maintained. A more difficult variation of the leg raises are slam-downs, where the legs are elevated as high as possible and forced downward to the floor by a partner.

119

Leg Raises

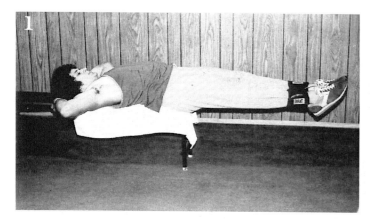

Leg raises (a).

Elevate legs.

Leg raises (b).

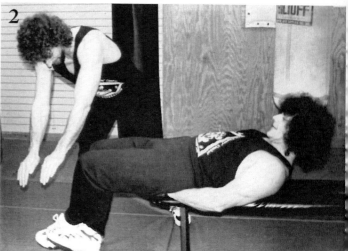

Push legs down.

Medicine Ball Drills

To toughen the stomach region and at the same time simulate getting hit there, a medicine ball is used in modern pankration training. Weighing 15 pounds or more, it is thrown forcefully by a partner against the front or side of the midsection. To vary this drill, lie on your back and have a partner drop the ball on your stomach. If training alone, you can drop on the ball with your stomach while doing push-ups.

Medicine ball toss.

Medicine ball drop.

Medicine ball side slams.

121

Medicine ball push-ups.

Weight Training for Upper-Body Strength

Grappling effectiveness, as well as punching power, is dependent on leverage and the combined effort of various muscles, namely the forearms, triceps, pectorals (chest), and deltoids (shoulders). Prior to the delivery of a blow or application of a grip or takedown, each set of muscles is in a relaxed state; they are instantly contracted at the exact moment of contact. The stronger muscle produces a faster, more responsive contraction, which, in turn, results in a more forceful action.

An excellent weight-training exercise for the forearm muscles is the reverse curl. The reverse curl works on the outside and top of the forearm, the lower portion of the arm that provides the "driving" force for many of the punching techniques employed in this fighting art. A special bar, called an E-Z Curl bar, is an absolute must for this exercise to really lock all the action into the forearms. The angles of the bar isolate the forearm muscles, forcing them to work synergistically so that only forearm strength and muscle perform the exercise.

Reverse curl.

Another forearm developer is the wrist roll. The equipment used for this tough exercise is a 10-pound weight attached to a cylindrical handle by a rope or cord. The length of the cord is such that the weight is at the level of the thighs when completely unwound. The trainee stands erect, with his arms raised straight out and the elbows locked, palms down, holding the handle horizontally. The elbows are not bent at any time. Without the arms moving, the cord is then wound up steadily on the handle by using only a wrist action. Both hands must raise the weight equally. Once the weight touches the hands, the cord is slowly unwound to lower the weight.

Wrist roll.

To develop the inside of the forearms, leverage bar rotations are considered the best method. Using a dumbbell weighted on one end and an overhand grip, the trainee twists his wrist back and forth.

The triceps, muscles located on the outer side of the upper arm, are also essential in punching and many grappling techniques. This muscle group is the one used in pushing movements, and since the muscle involved in punching is the same as in pushing, exercises to develop this area are commonplace in pankration training. The best triceps exercise is dips. Using parallel bars, drop your body slowly and then press upward. The legs are bent at all times, and the body is held erect.

Since the dip is essentially a triceps developer, be careful to maintain the proper form. If you lean forward too much, for example, it becomes a strict pectoral (chest) workout. Always give it the full repetition, going all the way up and down. The more fully the movement is made, the more fully the muscle is developed.

Dips.

Leverage bar rotations.

Elevated push-ups (triceps).

The bench press is for the chest and triceps.

The behind-the-neck press is good for the deltoids.

Flies are an effective chest exercise.

BASIC DRILLS

Breakfalls and Rolling Exercises

Practice in breaking a fall and rolling is essential to grapplers. It teaches the martial artist to soften the shock of falling when the body's balance is lost. It is also a means of using the force movement of the opponent, following its direction while avoiding the resistance of the ground. The most common breaking and rolling exercises are illustrated on the following pages.

Simple Back Fall

Crouch at the knees and let yourself roll gently back. Strike the mat forcefully with your arms just before your back hits the mat. Your head should *not* hit the mat.

Starting pose.   *Bend the knees.*

Fall back.   *Slap the mat.*

Simple Side Fall

Raise one leg, pivoting to the side, and roll back on your buttocks. Slap the mat hard with your nearest arm just prior to your back hitting the mat.

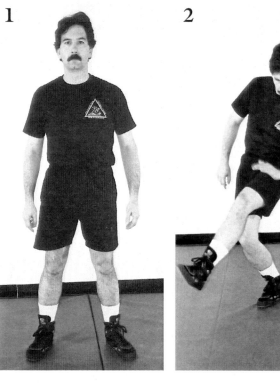

Starting pose.   *Raise the leg to the side.*

Slap the mat.

Simple Forward Fall

Drop gently to your knees and then fall forward. Slap the mat with your hands and forearms. Keep your hands directly in front of your face and the elbows turned slightly outward. Only the toes, knees, and forearms should touch the mat.

1

Starting pose.

2

Bend forward.

3

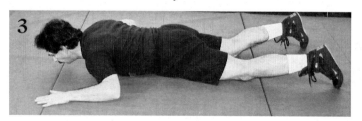

Fall forward and slap the mat.

Basic Forward Roll

With feet shoulder-width apart, place your left hand straight in front of you, with the right slightly behind it. Distribute your weight onto your left foot and left hand. Raise your right foot and roll down your left arm, onto the shoulder, back, and right side, slapping the mat with the right arm and leg at the completion of the fall.

1   **2**

Starting pose.   *Bend forward.*

3

Roll down the left arm.

4

Fall to the shoulder.

5

Slap the mat.

Spinning drill.

Spinning Drill

The spinning drill develops agility and quick, nimble movement for the pankratiast once he has secured top control on the ground. For the spinning drill, have a partner maintain a stationary position with his hands and knees planted on the mat and his head held low. Plant your chest and full weight directly on your partner's back, with legs well spread and toes touching the mat. Extend the arms outward. Once the command "spin" is given, rotate your body using your chest to pivot on your partner's back. You never cross your legs while spinning, nor do your hands make contact with your partner's body. Your partner randomly alternates lifting his arms to block your direction, forcing you to rotate the other way.

Skiamachia

Skiamachia is an ancient form of freestyle shadowboxing, which was popular among both Greek boxers and pankratiasts. It is used primarily to practice upright fighting skills, such as punching combinations, footwork, kicking, and defenses. The modern practitioner often uses a mirror, thereby reflecting his own image as a target or imaginary opponent. The mirror is particularly helpful in examining movements for such flaws as telegraphing blows.

Skiamachia improves form, balance, speed, and coordination, as opposed to a powerful punch. Since the trainee is striking the air and not a solid object, he must be careful not to hyperextend his limbs when executing his techniques, or injuries will result. In addition, the practitioner must be creative and spontaneous. Skiamachia is not in any way a prearranged form where memorization and strict mechanical precision are critical to execution. The emphasis is more like that in Greek dance, with freedom of expression and fluid, unplanned movement the key factors. Such practice better enables him to react instinctively to the uncertainties faced in an actual combat situation.

This training is timed in 3-minute rounds with 1-minute breaks. If performed properly, shadow-boxing can also benefit the cardiovascular system.

Skiamachia (punch in mirror).

Offense-Defense Drills

In these drills, a student attacks with various offensive techniques while his partner defends without retaliation. Both strikes and takedown attempts are employed in an attack. The defender can execute any defensive action, be it a parry against a punch, a block against a kick, or a sprawl against a leg tackle.

Sparring

Sparring, or free-fighting, with full contact and protective gear heads the list on the mu tau/pankration training plan. There is really no better practice in developing proficiency in combat. Sparring serves as the "testing ground" for techniques and for one's ability to withstand punishment. Only this type of activity offers the practitioner a realistic opportunity (second only to actual combat) to express and explore himself and to discover what works and what doesn't. It is the best means of keeping skills and reflexes fine-tuned.

There are various types of sparring advocated in a modern pankration palaistra, ranging from pyx (boxing) to open sparring sessions. At this level, pankratiasts go at it with few restrictions. The participants wear protective gear and are encouraged to hit and kick from shin to head, and to freely apply grappling and groundfighting techniques once they have closed. The duration of a free-sparring match is arranged in advance by both fighters or their trainer. A boundary, such as a circle on a matted floor, is normally used to contain the fighters. Because this is not treated as a contest, there are no points awarded, no referees, and no declaration of a winner. A match can be terminated at any time by a verbal surrender, a hard knockdown from a strike or throw, or a tapping-out to any submission hold. The sparmates realize well ahead of time that this training is a type of experimental analysis that attempts, as closely as possible, to duplicate the potential conditions of combat in either the ring or street.

To minimize the risk of serious injury, modern pankrati-

Protective gear.

asts wear headgear, mouthpieces, and groin cups, as well as special fight gloves with fingers to facilitate grappling techniques. Knee padding is also worn to protect the knees from abrasions often incurred during ground fighting.

The exhausting and grueling effect this training has on the human body cannot be denied. However, this is representative of mu tau's insistence on properly preparing a strong, well-conditioned athlete for combat. And those entering this phase with some irrational image of invincibility quickly discover their error. Everyone who spars under modern pankration conditions will be hit, kicked, and taken down. The goal is to minimize the effect of each of these actions while maximizing those of your own. A student quickly discovers how to adapt to a fight's unpredictability, while testing his knowledge, courage, and physical attributes. For those who undertake the study of the art, this is the foremost learning experience.

Shin block the leg kick.

Standing punch.

Elbowing on the ground.

Headlock and striking on the ground.

Sparring is an absolute necessity for those who compete in limited-rules fighting events. Following is a listing of the major variations of mu tau sparring practices.

I. **Pyx**
   (boxing)
   - Offensive techniques: Punching blows only to body and head
   - Defensive techniques: Parries and evasions
   - Match duration: Continuous fighting (2 minutes minimum)
   - Protective gear: Amphotides, 16-ounce gloves, mouthpiece, groin cup

II. **Laktisma pyxmachia**
   (kickboxing)
   - Offensive techniques: Punching blows to body and head; kicks to legs, body, and head
   - Defensive techniques: Parries, evasions, and shin blocks
   - Duration: Continuous fighting (2 minutes minimum)
   - Protective gear: Amphotides, 16-ounce gloves, mouthpiece, shin guards, groin cup

III. **Kato pale**
   (submission grappling)
   - Offensive techniques: Throws and takedowns; submission arm and leg locks; chokes
   - Defensive techniques: Reversals and escapes; sprawl
   - Other skills: Neck clinches and waist locks; shoots
   - Duration: Continuous fighting (2 minutes minimum)
   - Protective gear: Mouthpiece, kneepads

IV. **Ano pankration**
   (total stand-up fighting)
   - Offensive techniques: Punching to head and body; kicks to legs, body, and head; elbow strikes to head; knees to head and body; takedowns and throws; standing chokes
   - Defensive techniques: Parries and evasions; shin blocks; sprawl, reversals and escapes
   - Other skills: Neck clinches and waist locks; shoots
   - Duration: Continuous fighting (2 minutes minimum)
   - Protective gear: Amphotides, 16-ounce gloves, mouthpiece, groin cup, and shin guards

V. **Kato pankration**
   (open sparring—standing and ground)
   - Offensive techniques: Standing punches to head or body only; standing kicks to legs, body, and head; standing knees to head and body; standing elbows to head; takedowns and throws; ground submissions including arm and leg locks, chokes, and strikes to body (punches and knees)
   - Defensive techniques: Parries and evasions, shin blocks; sprawl; reversals and escapes
   - Other skills: Shoots, mounting and guard ground positions
   - Duration: Continuous fighting (2 minutes minimum)
   - Protective gear: Amphotides, spheres, mouthpiece, groin cup, shin guards, and kneepads

MODERN PANKRATION TERMINOLOGY

The following are some of the primary Greek and English terms spoken in a modern pankration training facility.

academy: School, training gym, institute.

adaptability: The ability to react spontaneously to meet the ever-changing, unpredictable conditions of combat.

advantage, position of: In grappling, having the top-mounted position on the opposing fighter.

agkohnizein: Greek for elbow strike.

aggressor: A classification of fighter who continually leads and presses the offensive action.

ahareeos: Greek for novice or beginning student.

aidos: Honorable sportsmanship without arrogance.

akoniti: Greek term for a "walkover" victory (no contest).

amphotides: Greek term for headgear; helmets worn in sparring practice by ancient pankratiasts to protect the head from injury.

angling: A tactical positioning of the body in relation to that of the opponent. This positioning is a crucial factor in delivering a successful attack. The *angle of entry*, as it is often called, can be of three variations: straight on, flank (inside/outside), and rear.

ano pankration: Upright fighting similar to kickboxing that specializes in striking techniques with fists, feet, elbows, and knees.

arete: A Greek concept including the attributes of honor, nobility, and virtue.

arheegos: Greek for master trainer.

audio perception: The ability to anticipate an unseen, surprise action through a highly developed sense of hearing. It is often enhanced by blindfolded training drills.

back mount: Ground control position with the top fighter straddled on top of his opponent's back.

balance: The physical attribute that enables an athlete to maintain good alignment both in a static position and during motion.

battlefield pankration: Refer to *panmachia*.

blitzing: Any swift, abrupt, inward rush that is usually accompanied by a barrage of heavy punches or a takedown.

body blasting: A heavy, concentrated punching assault on an opponent's midsection.

bob and weave: An up-and-down, side-to-side swaying motion of the shoulders and head employed at close range combat that is both defensive and aggressive in nature. It makes the fighter extremely difficult to hit squarely and adds power to his short punches (hooks and uppercuts).

broken rhythm: A sudden, unexpected variation in offense either in the form of a change of direction or altering the set pace (rhythm) with which the techniques are made. Results in a disruption in the opponent's sense of timing.

blocking: Taking a blow on the arms, shoulders, or shins.

body banging: A training drill for hardening the torso through the use of padded gloves or a medicine ball.

breakdown: A grappling move in which the fighter flattens an opponent to the ground on his stomach or side, usually when he is in the bottom position.

bridging the gap: An expression commonly employed for closing the spatial relationship (distance) between fighters in order to land a blow or execute a takedown. Bridging the gap and attacking are generally simultaneous actions.

cadence: Speed regulated to coincide with that of the opponent. It is a specific rhythm at which a succession of movements is executed.

caestus: An addition by the Romans to their combat sports events. It essentially armed the boxers with a lethal spiked and weighted glove, which replaced the athletic skill inspired by the Greeks with an increase in brutality and death.

central vision: A type of visual focusing in which the eyes and attention are fixed on one point.

chambering: Bringing the leg to the cocked position just prior to kicking to attain maximum speed and power in the kick's delivery.

chancery: A popular ancient pankration technique involving the pulling of the hair to gain leverage for one's blows or gaining release from a grappling hold.

classical way: A traditional martial arts system that remains fixed in time and does not flow with the constant change of our progressive culture.

clinch: At close range, grabbing the opponent by the legs, waist, or around the neck. Usually is a starting point for knee strikes or grappling action.

combination: A fluid sequence of two or more blows or strategic attacks.

combos: Slang for combinations.

complementing force: Flowing in the direction that the force is being generated rather than against it. Often applied in grappling situations and on defense.

complex attack: Not a simple maneuver but one requiring more energy and movements, such as any spinning-type attack.

control: The authority or power to regulate or dominate a situation, such as a grappling hold or the course of a fight itself.

core techniques: Refers to the major tools of the system that distinguish it from other martial arts. For example, the *klimakismos* and *gastrizein* are considered some of the core techniques of pankration.

counter: A blow or grappling technique given in response to an opponent's lead. Another of the recognized mu tau pankration methods of strategically deploying the tools.

cover: Raising the arms to protect against hooking punches to the head.

critical distance: The range at which an attack *must* be made.

critical target: A vulnerable spot of the human anatomy that, when correctly struck, causes the greatest damage to an opponent. The eyes and groin are examples of critical targets.

cross-step: A type of offensive footwork used to deliver certain mu tau pankration kicking tools.

croucher: A fighter who does battle with his stance lowered and his upper body bent forward.

curved line: The path taken for circular-type blows, such as hooking punches and kicks.

darting: Rapid, crisp, in and out moves usually for scoring quick jabs.

deception: A decoy or false movement used to elicit a response from an opponent. Applied in an indirect attack.

deflection: A sharp, well-timed slap of the palm to the inside, outside, or onto an oncoming blow or kick, to divert the assault from its original path.

disciple: A follower or student of the art.

distancing: The amount of space between fighters.

distraction: See deception.

dodging: an evasive form of footwork involving lateral movement, to the inside or outside of an oncoming blow.

double-leg takedown: A takedown maneuver where both of the opponent's legs are gripped.

ducking: A defensive evasion for escaping hooks and swings to the head by dropping the body forward.

efficiency: A technique that is functional without wasting energy or movement.

elevator: An escape move employed against a top-mounted opponent that features arching of the back and legs when the fighter is trapped on the bottom.

elusive: A constantly moving target that is difficult to hit or take down to the ground.

endurance: The ability of the body to perform work over long periods.

endyma: Greek for training outfit.

environmental training: Training that deals with acclimating the student with his surroundings when engaged in combat.

erroso: Verbal greeting expressed as part of *hereteesmos* to a fellow student or an instructor.

escape: Gaining a neutral position after being controlled in a grappling position or hold.

etimi: Greek for ready.

explosiveness: The action of abruptly bursting forth or releasing energy from a prior state of relative calm.

extrapolate: To tactically predict an opponent's response to a certain move on the basis of previous responses to the same movement.

evasion: To avoid an oncoming blow or kick by a precisely timed head, body, or foot movement, thereby allowing the hands to be free to retaliate.

fakes: Body gestures—such as movements of the eyes, head or shoulders—used to disguise an intended attack.

fall: In sport pankration, the moment when an opponent's shoulders touch the ground from a throw or takedown.

feint: A pretense of attacking one area and delivering the actual blow to another by means of false limb movements (e.g., hand and foot feints).

flank: Angling one's body to the inside or outside position of the opponent's front foot.

fluidity: The capability of performing techniques smoothly and with the utmost ease.

focus: Zeroing in on a small target area with a maximum of force.

follow-through: Driving the fist or foot internally, several inches beyond the target area. Mu tau pankration blows vary in depth or follow-through.

four-three: A close range punching combination made up of an uppercut followed by a hook.

freestyle wrestling: An open style of amateur wrestling that allows the contestants the full use of their bodies to score points or pin their opponent.

gastrizein: Greek for stomach kick.

gonato: Greek for knee.

gonatizein: Greek for striking with the knee.

grappling: Another term for wrestling. It consists of take-downs, joint locks, submission chokeholds, and other maneuvers.

Greco-Roman wrestling: A major style of wrestling used in international competition as well as the Olympic Games in which the use of the feet or legs is limited.

guard: (1) The placement of the arms in the readiness position, or (2) a defensive position on the ground in which the fighter's legs are scissored about the opponent's waist, restricting his offensive ability from the top mount.

gymnastes: In ancient Greece, an athletic trainer.

half-committed thrust: A partially executed blow employed to evoke a response from an opponent; akin to feinting.

headhunter: A striker who delivers his blows solely to the head.

head shot: A blow aimed at the head.

heart: Refers to a fighter's inner drive to win at all costs.

heave: An ancient grappling technique sometimes used to counter a leg takedown. It involves gripping the opponent about the waist, lifting him, and dropping him on his head.

heavy artillery: Mu tau pankration's arsenal of full-powered penetrating blows and kicks.

hellanodikes: Greek for official or referee.

hereteesmos: Greek for salutation.

high line: The area of the human anatomy above shoulder level.

himantes: Hand wraps of soft oxhide worn by ancient Greek boxers.

itona: The top of the instructor's endyma.

oplomachia: Greek for fighting with weapons.

oplomachos: Greek for weapons specialist.

yptiasmos: Greek for back-fall.

infighting: Combat action at close quarters. Elbowing, knee-ing, and grappling techniques are favored offensive weapons at this range.

initiation speed: The rapidity with which a technique or movement is triggered from readiness.

inside hand range: The distance from which compact, bent-arm hand blows are delivered.

interception: A blow or kick delivered as the opponent is in the process of launching a blow of his own.

isolated sparring: A developmental type of sparring drill that restricts the participants to a certain technique or set of techniques.

jamming: A means of obstructing a kicking attempt by sens-ing the impending attack and then moving in close before the kick has had any real chance of gaining any impetus. It is especially effective against the fighter who emphasizes kicks in his offense.

joint lock: A grappling technique featuring any type of painful grip or hold upon the opponent's joints (e.g., wrist, elbow, knee, ankle).

kato pale: Greek for ground wrestling.

kato pankration: A rougher and more comprehensive com-ponent of the sport emphasizing everything-goes ground combat. This is the form preferred in the ancient Olympic Games.

keereeos: Greek for patriarch. This title is reserved for found-ing grandmaster of modern Greek martial art.

klimakismos: Greek for ladder trick. A grappling maneuver where a fighter jumps on his opponent's back and applies a choke while scissoring his abdomen at the same time.

klimax: An agreement between fighters to trade blows with-out blocking them until one fighter dropped and a clear-cut winner was declared.

KO: Short for knock-out. This refers to rendering an oppo-nent unconscious by a blow, kick, or grappling assault.

korykeoin: A special room in the palaestra equipped with train-ing apparatus for boxers and pankratiasts.

korykos: Greek for suspended heavy bags.

laktisma: Greek for kicking/striking with the foot.

laktisma pyxmachia: Greek for kickboxing.

latent distraction: A distractive body or limb movement com-posed of feints and fakes.

lateral movement: Refers to sidestepping or dodging.

lead: The initial attack. It is normally a characteristic of the more aggressive fighter.

left stancer: See orthodox position.

level: Refers to either *ano* (standing) or *kato* (ground) com-bat.

leverage: Positioning the body in such a manner that the greatest amount of physical force can be generated into the blow or grappling maneuver.

linear movement: Straightforward or backward movement (i.e., advancing/retreating).

low line: The area of the human anatomy from the waist down.

long range: The distance beyond arm's reach of an adversary in which kicks are the most effective offensive weapons.

luring: See drawing.

mahitiki tehni: Greek for martial art.

manifest distraction: Any unexpected noise resulting in a momentary reduction in body coordination.

midline: The area of the anatomy from waist level to the shoulders.

MMA: Abbreviation for mixed martial arts. Pankration and mu tau are considered the forerunners of the mixed martial arts movement today.

mobility: Continual, unpredictable movement. It applies to footwork and upper body motion (bob and weave).

momentum: The product of the mass (weight) and velocity of a moving body. It is also referred to as *impetus*.

mount: The top-control position assumed in ground fighting.

MTP: An abbreviation for mu tau pankration.

mu tau: A term coined in 1970 from the anglicized pronunciation of two Greek letters to represent modern Greek martial art. Symbolically, the letters converted to their English equivalents "m" and "t" are an acronym for *mahitiki tehni*, the native Greek term that literally means *martial art*.

NHB: Abbreviation for no-holds-barred fighting.

nonclassical: Not saturated with traditional theory and ritual; progressive and ever changing.

O-D drills: Drills wherein one trainee attacks and the other concentrates solely on defense.

Olympic pankration: The combat sport of the ancient Olympic Games that allowed any offensive technique other than gouging and biting.

one-four: A numbering scheme for a jab lead and uppercut combination.

one-four-three: A three-punch series of lead jab, uppercut, and hook.

one-three: Another numbered punching combination for a hook punch off a jab lead.

one-two: A numbering scheme for a jab and reverse-thrust punching combination.

one-two-three: A numbered three-punch combination for a jab, rear thrust, and hook punch.

orthia pale: Greek for upright wrestling; also referred to as *orthopale*. It includes clinching, takedowns, and throwing

techniques.

orthodox position: A position of combat readiness in which the left hand and left foot are placed forward.

outfighting: See long range.

outside hand range: The distance from which straightline punches, such as the lead jab and reverse thrust, are employed.

pacing: A means of actively (physically and mentally) regulating the output of energy during the course of doing combat or running long distances.

palaistra: Greek for training hall, wrestling school, or competition boundary.

paidotribes: In ancient Greece, a trainer in unarmed combat.

pale: Greek term for wrestling.

pammachon: A variant of *panmachia*.

panmachia: Greek for total fight; an old term for integrated unarmed combat used primarily on the battlefield prior to the sport of pankration. Sometimes referred to as "battlefield pankration."

pankration: Literally translated in Greek as "all powers." An ancient Greek combat sport that was introduced into the Olympic Games of 648 B.C. It is the primary foundation upon which the art of mu tau evolved.

parathesis: Sideways stance used primarily for punching.

parry: See deflection.

partiality: An inclination to favoring "this" over "that," such as straight lines over curves, kicking over striking, etc. It implies the inability to comprehend "total fighting freedom."

passive blocking: A classical defense (seen in Asian karate styles) in which hard, rigid blocks are performed with one arm while the other arm is placed passively at the hip.

penetration: See follow-through.

peripheral vision: Visual focusing in combat whereby the eyes are fixed on one point as attention expands to a greater area.

pile driver: See heave.

pivot: Turning the body to attain maximum power in one's blows. Various pivoting maneuvers are employed for specific MTP techniques, such as hook punching and back-leg round kicks.

polymeestees: Greek for warrior.

polemikos: Greek for "one who fights"; a combat athlete.

positioning: Refers to the placement of the head and limbs in the on-guard fighting pose.

pothee: Greek for foot.

preparation: Readying oneself both mentally and physically for unrestrained combat conditions.

primary tools: The most fundamental techniques of the art.

probing: Investigating and analyzing the opponent's reactions through exploratory actions.

progressive: Nonclassical; modern; constantly evolving with fresh ideas relative to combat realism.

pygmis: Greek term for punch.

pulsating rhythm: A perpetual movement that recurs alternately or in regulated sequence. It is developed chiefly through training to music.

pyrrhic: In ancient Greece, dancelike exercises practiced with weaponry that resembled actual fighting movements.

pyxmachia: Greek for boxing; also referred to as *pyx*.

rassein apaly: Greek terminology for "bring to ground." It applies to takedowns, throws, and sweeps.

reaction speed: The rapidity with which physical responses are made to an opponent's moves.

readiness: A state of super alertness from the guard position.

recovery: The action of coming back strong after an initial attack has landed.

reflex action: Instantaneous response, without thinking, to an opponent's physical actions.

release: Escaping from a grappling hold or submission technique.

retreat: To back away from an attack.

reversal: In grappling, the altering of a control situation.

riding: Refers to controlling an opponent from the top position.

right stancer: See southpaw position.

roadwork: A running technique used to develop stamina.

rollout: In grappling, an escape move by which you roll rapidly with force in the same direction that your opponent's weight is concentrated.

roots: The early beginnings or foundation upon which a progressive art is based. For example, early pankration concepts are the roots of MTP.

rotating movement: Circling one's adversary in a tactical process of probing for openings and changing angles.

round: A fighting period, lasting 2 or 3 minutes in duration.

runner: The classification of a fighter who continually hits and retreats.

setups: A series of preliminary actions, including feints, that lead into major attacks.

set patterns: Prearranged training drills, such as kata and one-step/two-step sparring. They are characteristic of the classical Asian martial arts.

"sharpening the tools": Improving the speed, power, and accuracy of one's techniques through regular training. It involves the use of various punching and kicking equipment.

shifty: A movement characteristic of the fighter skilled in lateral movement.

shoot: An offensive maneuver characterized by dropping one's center of gravity and tackling an opponent's legs.

shuffle: Moving on the balls of the feet; not flat-footed.

side mount: Ground control position where the fighter on top is to the side of his opponent.

single-leg takedown: A takedown attempt in which the assault is directed toward only one of the opponent's legs.

skiamachia: Greek for shadow-fighting. A favored form of training by ancient Greek boxers and pankratiasts, it is the practice of fighting moves without an opponent.

slide: An offensive type of footwork where the rear foot "hops" inward, thereby bridging the gap suddenly and swiftly.

slipping: Avoiding a blow by moving the head to the left or right without moving the body out of range.

southpaw: The ready position in which the right hand and foot are placed forth.

spacing: See distancing.

Spartan pankration: A no-holds-barred form of sport pankration that allowed biting and gouging, practiced exclusively by the Spartans.

spheres: Greek for fight gloves.

sprawl: A rapid evasive maneuver to avoid being grasped by the legs. It is initiated when the opposing fighter dives in low to attempt a takedown.

springiness: A quality of combat movement made possible by slightly bending the knees and raising the heels.

stamina: See endurance.

stamahta: Greek for halt or stop.

stance: The positioning of the lower body (feet and legs) in the ready pose.

step-through: Offensive footwork used in the delivery of specific mu tau pankration kicks.

strategy: A mental planning of actions or maneuvers used to gain an edge over an opponent. It also is a quality of an intelligent fighter.

striking range: The fighting distance from which blows and kicks can reach an opponent's critical targets.

submission hold: A lock or hold on an opponent's neck or joints that forces him to surrender or suffer strangulation or a broken limb. Such a technique is cause for terminating an all-out sparring match.

survival instinct: An internal drive that is not easily learned and that results in an attitude to win at all costs. Compare to heart.

swaying movement: See bobbing and weaving.

sustained attack: To keep up or maintain a steady offensive onslaught, usually with the same technique.

systasis: Greek for square-on stance. It is used mainly in kicking.

tactics: Well-planned actions and steps taken to ultimately conquer the opposition. The term refers to the strategic ability of a fighter to meet and solve problems as they arise in combat. They are not preconceived notions but are part of an on-going process that continues until the battle ends. They are primarily concerned with avoiding the opponent's strengths and exploiting his weaknesses.

tackle: See takedown.

takedown: A grappling technique whereby the opponent is knocked off his feet and placed in a helpless situation against a follow-up offensive.

telegraph: A signal of intended actions, such as a dropping of the shoulder or the windup of the arm prior to delivering a punch.

tempo: Refers to the rate of speed at which a fighter makes any physical or combat movement. Variation in tempo, such as a sudden speeding up of an attack, is often an effective tactic in catching the opponent off guard. Tempo is also applicable in such exercises such as running and jumping rope, where change of output is essential.

thaskalos: Greek for instructor.

theethaktor: Greek for senior trainer.

tie-up: See clinch.

timing: The sudden reaction or response to a stimulus. It includes the capability to seize the exact moment for executing an action.

toe-to-toe: A commonly used expression for infighting.

tools: A term used to encompass the diverse technical elements of the art. It can be broken down into hand tools, foot tools, infighting tools, and defensive tools.

torque: The capacity of a force for producing twisting or rotation, such as turning the hips into a power punch for greater striking impact. Compare with leverage.

totality: Not partial in nature, as in a "style," but including all ways and means to carry out an objective.

transition: Closing the distance from one specified range to another. For instance, making the transition from punching range to grappling range. It also applies to such "level" changes as going from stand-up to ground fighting.

trap: Holding down and checking the use of an opponent's arm so it cannot be employed for purposes of offense and defense.

trip: A takedown finish in which the opponent's leg or foot is blocked or kicked out from under him.

unpredictability: Making all physical actions a surprise to an opponent; never doing something in an expected manner.

velocity: The speed with which an object, such as the hand, foot, or body, moves in a specified direction.

visual perception: The ability to use trained eyesight to gauge distance, uncover open targets upon which to score, and detect aggressive actions and moves before they can impart damage.

voeethos: Greek for associate trainer.

vulnerable point: Refers to any area of the body prone to disabling results when struck precisely. Compare to critical target.

zone: A section of the body used as a target for one's blows and kicks. Refers to high, medium, and low lines.

GREEK NUMBERS (1-10)

1—*ena*   6—*eksi*

2—*theo*   7—*efta*

3—*tria*   8—*octo*

4—*tesera*   9—*ennaya*

5—*pende*   10—*theka*

MODERN PANKRATION RANKINGS

Unlike karate, tae kwon do, and kung fu, colored belts are not worn to indicate rank in modern Hellenic martial art. In ancient Greek combat sport, a practitioner was considered either a student (*ahareeos*), a competing fighter (*polymeestees*), or a teacher (*paidotribes*). In mu tau pankration, however, a unique ranking system based on experience, athletic skill, and dedication is implemented. Various physical skills (e.g., positioning, movement, striking, grappling, defenses, fight strategy) and knowledge of the history and concepts of the system are tested at each grade level (GL) as a prerequisite for promotion. The rankings are classified as follows.

Ahareeos (beginner/novice): GL 1–4

Polymeestees (warrior): GL 5–6

Paidotribes (trainer)

GL 7	*voeethos* (assistant trainer)
GL 8	*thaskalos* (instructor)
GL 9	*theethaktor* (senior instructor)
GL 10	*arheegos* (master)

Keereeos (founding grandmaster): GL 11

ARETE

Arete is an ancient Greek term that is difficult to explain within the context of the English language. Essentially it included the concepts of excellence, nobility, valor, honor, and virtue. It was a goal to be sought by every citizen of Hellas, and past pankration champions, such as Arrichion and Dioxippus, possessed these qualities to a high degree. Many believed that the gods bestowed them as gifts to selected mortals.

In modern Hellenic martial art, arete refers to the dynamics that shape technique and the inner attributes that separate the great martial artist or champion athlete from the average one. It can include anything from a blow that is felt but not seen to one's resistance to accepting defeat at the hands of his adversary. Arete is certainly more than just physical skills; it also embraces mental characteristics that elevate an individual to the realm of superiority in his chosen craft.

PHYSICAL ARETE

Strength
Strength refers to the effort that can be exerted with a single maximal muscle contraction.

Strength is definitely an asset to the MTP fighter, especially during close-range combat. Success in grappling is frequently the result of the effective use of one's strength.

Speed is developed by specialized weight training and heavy-bag workouts.

Speed
Speed comprises the following elements: quickness of the eye to spot openings; quickness of mind to select the right move at the proper time; quickness of reflexive action to react explosively and without hesitation; and quickness of hand and foot in executing the chosen technique instantly and effectively.

- Economy of motion and relaxed muscles enhance speed. Wasted movements, overall tension, and unnecessary muscular contractions reduce speed and dissipate energy.
- Speed in hitting refers to how fast a blow covers distance to get to its target. It includes sudden initiation (no telegraphing) and maximum acceleration up to the moment of impact. Regardless of distance, the final phase of the striking movement should be the fastest.
- Speed is instantaneous. Any deliberation in movements is definitely detrimental to speed potential.
- Speed development drills include the use of the platform bag, double-end bag, focus gloves, and various sparring activities.

3. **Power**
- Power is a combination of strength and speed. It implies the ability to develop fast, explosive movements against resistance.
- Power is dependent on leverage and positioning of the body in such a way that it drives the blow, kick, or grappling maneuver. It is not the product of mere arm or leg strength alone.
- Power is enforced by tensing the working muscles at the moment of impact and not a second before.
- It is essential that the various muscle groups and tendons involved in the movement are kept loose and relaxed

prior to contact. If the muscles are already tense, they cannot be further contracted when impact is made. Tensing either too early or too late diminishes hitting force.

- A powerful blow is a penetrating one. It goes "through" the target, not just to it! The idea is to focus on "driving" the fist or foot several inches behind the target, utilizing mind and body together.
- Power-development drills make use of the korykos, kick pads, etc.

4. Coordination

- Coordination refers to the synchronized interaction between the body's nervous and muscular systems. This function is important for producing skillful movement.
- The well-coordinated fighter performs his techniques smoothly and gracefully. He makes purposeful actions with a minimum of effort and a maximum of speed and power.
- Efficient movement is a matter of training the nervous system to send impulses to certain muscles, causing them to contract while halting impulses to the antagonistic muscles simultaneously, allowing them to relax. Properly coordinated impulses surge with the exact intensity required to attain skill.
- We learn solely by doing. By forming proper connections in the nervous system through constant practice, the more familiar we become with the action. Greater familiarity results in a higher skill level.

5. Flexibility

- Flexibility is the range of possible motion in a joint or series of joints.
- Flexibility is developed through proper stretching exercises and contributes to better athletic performance while decreasing the risk of injury, such as muscle strains and pulls.
- It is beneficial to precede flexibility exercises with endurance training.
- Flexibility has been proven to improve when there is an elevation in the internal temperature of the body, which results from endurance training.

6. Timing

- Timing is the sudden reaction to a stimulus. It includes the ability to realize the right moment for executing an action.
- Timing is best exemplified by a movement that is initiated without obvious preparation and proceeds smoothly without deliberation so that it succeeds in hitting the opponent before he is alerted and has a chance to defend.
- The exact moment of launching an offensive must be seized instinctively. For example, a blow should be made when the opponent's concentration is misdirected or when he is deceived out of position.

- Reaction time is affected immensely by a fighter's psychological and physiological conditions. Being properly warmed up also has some effect.
- Movement time is the time taken to perform a single-arm or -leg technique or foot manipulation. Such timing varies according to the speed of each trainee.
- Timing a blow is a critical ingredient of powerful hitting. A good pankratiast attempts to beat his opponent to the attack by taking the initiative and forcing the reaction of his foe. This is best accomplished by hitting the foe as he moves in, is lured into moving in (drawing), or prepares to launch an attack.
- Speed, both physically and mentally, is the essence of timing. When applied at the opportune moment, speed (together with shrewd judgment) ensures the success of any offensive or defensive technique.
- The initiation of a technique's execution is of primary relevance in the consideration of timing. Unlike baseball players or golfers who take practice swings to commence their particular movements, the fighter must react in an instant. A failure in timing could be disastrous.

7. Accuracy

- Accuracy is the quality of landing precise blows on an intended target.
- No matter how potentially destructive a blow or kick is, it is ineffective if it does not land on the "mark."
- Accuracy requires a familiarity with the vital points of the human anatomy (e.g., eyes, neck, solar plexus, ribs, thigh, shin).

8. Endurance

- Endurance is the capability of the body to resist fatigue while performing a prolonged, relatively strenuous activity.
- There are two distinct types of endurance: muscular and cardiovascular.
- Muscular endurance is the quality of the muscles to remain strong and in a constant state of relaxation over extended periods. Cardiovascular endurance (stamina) is the quality of the heart, lungs, and circulatory system to function effectively for prolonged intervals.
- Cardiovascular endurance training is of the aerobic type and involves the large musculature of the lower limbs. Running, biking, jumping rope, bagwork for 3 minutes, and sparring are all excellent exercises for this purpose.

9. Agility

- Agility is the ability to quickly and nimbly change the direction of the movement of the body. In combat, an agile fighter is one who can continually frustrate the offensives attempted by his opponent.

10. Balance

- Balance refers to the control of one's center of gravity during moving, attacking, and defending. Proper bal ance is necessary in the execution of kicking, striking, and grappling techniques.

- Balance must be studied in motion, not from a rigid, immobile posture.
- Good balance is important for follow-up movements. Be careful of an overcommitment in penetrating attacks.

MIND ARETE

1. The Competitive Spirit

- The Greeks had the first true agonistic culture. Their love of competition was displayed in all they did, from sport to their excellence in warfare. Combat athletes possess this same fondness for testing themselves under the most challenging conditions. In the street, this mindset is turned up a notch because it is no longer a matter of winning and losing, but one of life or death. We call this the "killer instinct," that ability to survive at all costs, and it exists in all of us but at different levels. These levels exist in accordance with our personalities; the more aggressive types have the greater intensity to win, even if it means maiming his opponent.
- The worst enemies in combat are your own self-doubt and fear. You must conquer all negative thoughts and feelings of intimidation. You must give your all at every opportunity and demand more of your own capabilities than you feel is possible. Once a fight commences, you cannot question your chances. The outcome often depends on your determination.

2. Awareness

- Awareness of your surroundings in combat is essential to victory. You must attempt to out-think your rival and gain the most advantageous positions from which to attack.
- The goal is to exploit the weaknesses of your opponent while avoiding his strengths.
- Employ those tools that work best for you. Mount a relentless onslaught once you have your foe hurt or have him in obvious trouble.

3. The Ability to Take It

- Overcome the subconscious fear of getting hurt if hit. Condition the body to take shots there. Develop evasiveness to dissipate the force of blows directed to the head.
- In Spartan pankration's definition of streetfighting, one rule prevails: There are NO rules! Do anything you can to avoid being injured or maimed. It is the "kill or be killed" attitude that prevails here. Snapping the opponent's neck, ripping out his eye, or biting off his ear is all within the all-out philosophy of this martial art.
- Full-contact sparring is the best means of preparing for a streetfight, but it is only a simulation and not the exact same thing. Mu tau pankration training attempts to capture its essence, but the outcome of a sparring match is immensely different from that on the street.

SOME PANKRATION FACTOIDS

- Ancient Greek pankration does not appear in Homer's writings prior to the 5th century B.C. According to myth, pankration was the creation of either the great Attican hero Theseus, who killed the fierce Minotaur in the labyrinth with his striking and grappling skills, or Hercules, whose feats are legendary in the annals of Greek athletics.

- Pankration became the cornerstone of the ancient Olympic Games in 648 B.C. Considered one of the "heavy events," pankration was a simulation of an earlier battle-field form of unarmed combat called *panmachia*. The first Olympic pankration victor was Lygdamis of Syracuse.

- The Spartans elected not to compete in Olympic pankration but had their own version of the sport that permitted everything, including biting and gouging.

- Ancient sport pankration died out with the festivals of antiquity in A.D. 391 near the end of the Western Roman Period. Some of the reasons for its decline were "professionalism" that brought with it the loss of athletic excellence, the increasing violence of the competitions, and the growing power of Christianity, which forbade pagan worship.

- Some historians believe that pankration laid the groundwork for the development of Asian karate and kung fu as a result of Alexander the Great's invasion of the subcontinent in 326 B.C.

- Pankration was revived from its ashes as a modern combat sport and as a subset of Greek martial art in the late 1960s. It was taught in 1971 at the first Spartan Academy in the greater Boston area.

- Pankration was first exposed to mainstream martial arts when it was featured on the cover of *Black Belt* magazine in November 1973. It was among the very first contemporary "cross-training" or mixed martial arts styles practiced in the modern world.

- Greece, the motherland of pankration, did not restore its own version of the combat sport until the Hellenic Federation of Pankration Athlima was organized in 1995.

- Grandmaster Jim Arvanitis has been a consistent media presence for the past 30 years, having been featured in all the major martial arts publications. He was the first to write full-length books and be featured in videos devoted to pankration and the Hellenic combat arts. He is also a 14-time Hall of Fame inductee and is endorsed as the "father of modern pankration."

- Contrary to rumor, there is no Olympic pankration event scheduled for the 2004 Games in Athens, Greece. There are international tournaments being held, but they are not Olympic-sanctioned.

PANKRATION PRODUCTS

For the latest clothing, instructional media, and products bearing the trademarked logo of mu tau pankration, contact these official Web sites:

<www.mutau.net/pankration> (the Greek Martial Art Portal, considered the worldwide pankration informational resource)

<www.spartanacademy.com> (the foremost facility in the world for learning Greek martial art and modern pankration)

PARTING SHOTS OF PANKRATION TECHNIQUES

The photos on the remaining pages are representative of the "core" techniques and skills of both the classic and contemporary forms of Greek pankration depicted throughout this book.

Low round kick to the thigh.

Kick to the face from the ground.

Ano klimakismos.

Uppercut to the chin.

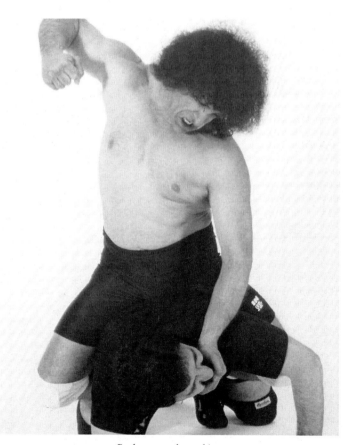

Back-mounted punching.

Exchanging kicks.

Side choke on the ground.

Armlock and elbow strike on the ground.

Armlock and punching on the ground.

Elbow lock from a side mount.

Knee kick to the face.

PARTING SHOTS OF PANKRATION TECHNIQUES

High front kick.

Lead straight punch to the face.

GRANDMASTER JIM ARVANITIS

Grandmaster Demetrios (Jim) Arvanitis is internationally renowned as the "father" of modern pankration. He took up the study of boxing (pyx) and Greco-Roman wrestling (pale) at an early age, and soon thereafter learned of the fighting sport of his ancestors called *pankration*. A driven athlete with strong ethnic ties, Jim made it his life's work to rebuild the ancient "all-powers" combat sport into a modern "cross-training" martial arts system.

To expand upon his unarmed skills, especially in the area of stand-up striking, Arvanitis studied a number of other styles including Muay Thai (Thai boxing) and French savate. He also worked extensively with established practitioners of combat judo. An avid reader, the dynamic Greek-American analyzed a number of other fighting methods. After years of research, Jim revived the ancient combat sport and developed the first contemporary Greek martial art, which he named *mu tau*. A unique composite of his previous studies, Arvanitis' system integrated modern techniques with principles modeled after those of his ancient forebears. It was Arvanitis who regenerated the extinct system, introduced it to the United States as early as 1971, and popularized it throughout the world in the years that followed.

Along with his almost fanatical obsession with training, Arvanitis is a highly respected historian, technician, and innovator. As a competitor, he had outstanding records in boxing and wrestling. Jim was also a seasoned streetfighter during his earlier years and was undefeated in impromptu challenge matches.

The mu tau founder has been featured in all of the top martial arts magazines, including *Inside Kung-Fu, Official*

Karate, Martial Arts and Combat Sports, Fighting Champions, Karate Illustrated, Martial Arts Masters, Jiu-Jitsu Grappling Guide, Inside Karate, Fighting Stars, American Karate, Martial Arts Ultimate Warriors, World of Martial Arts, and *Karate International.* He was also on the cover of *Black Belt* in 1973. The master pankratiast has made numerous television appearances, conducted seminars throughout the United States, Canada, and Europe, and is listed in the *Martial Arts Encyclopedia, Who's Who in American Martial Arts,* and *Martial Arts Founders & Masters* for his many accomplishments. Arvanitis also wrote previous books on his art in 1980 and 1997.

His film credits include starring in a pankration documentary and numerous instructional and training videos. Other physical feats include his now famous world record for the "thumb pushup," which he did using both arms and using only one arm.

Arvanitis is among the first to have been bestowed the title of grandmaster of the Hellenic martial arts and has received numerous Hall of Fame induction awards. He is a member of the prestigious World Head of Family Sokeship Council and was among the first inductees to *Action Martial Arts* magazine's "Academy Awards."

Arvanitis' students have included law enforcement personnel, bodyguards, and members of the military's elite special forces. Arvanitis was instrumental in preparing many U.S. Army ground troops for the Persian Gulf conflict.

Today Jim Arvanitis exemplifies the classic Spartan athlete by training religiously and following a special diet. Those who practice with him continue to be amazed by his speed, power, and fitness. As more than one partner has indicated, "holding pads for him to hit is a frightening experience—it is like being struck by a freight train." A full-time trainer and coach, Jim is in great demand at seminars throughout the world.

The innovative Arvanitis has combined natural athletic ability with a diligent work ethic to become the most famous martial arts practitioner of Greek ancestry in modern times. His efforts alone have been instrumental in reviving an ancient legacy, one which is believed to be the oldest mixed combat system on record.

WORLD'S LEADING MAGAZINE OF SELF-DEFENSE

BLACK BELT

17250
NOV. 1973
60 CENTS

CAPTURING THE ELUSIVE "INNER FORCE" OF THE MARTIAL ARTIST
The indestructible "ki" is the basis of the universe; developing it is an art in itself

THE UNCHAINED "KARATE" OF ANCIENT GREECE
All-out combat in an original Olympic sport

JAPANESE REGAIN HONOR AT 1973 WORLD JUDO CHAMPIONSHIPS
The competition was tougher than ever, but Kano's descendants were not to be denied

As featured on the cover of Black Belt *(1973).*

The superhuman single-arm thumb push-up.